Probation
and Parole

CRIME, JUSTICE, AND PUNISHMENT

Probation and Parole

Richard Worth

Austin Sarat, GENERAL EDITOR

CHELSEA HOUSE PUBLISHERS
Philadelphia

Frontispiece: *A parole hearing.*

Chelsea House Publishers
Editor in Chief Sally Cheney
Director of Production Kim Shinners
Production Manager Pamela Loos
Art Director Sara Davis
Senior Editor John Ziff
Production Editor Diann Grasse
Cover Design Keith Trego

Layout by 21st Century Publishing and
Communications, Inc., New York, N.Y.

First Printing

1 3 5 7 9 8 6 4 2

The Chelsea House World Wide Web address is
http://www.chelseahouse.com

Library of Congress Cataloging-in-Publication Data
CIP applied for ISBN 0-7910-5766-6

Contents

Fears and Fascinations:
   An Introduction to Crime,
   Justice, and Punishment
   Austin Sarat 7

1   Coping with Criminals:
     A Brief History 13

2   Probation 31

3   Parole 39

4   Juvenile Crime:
     Probation and Aftercare 55

5   Does Probation Work? 69

6   Evaluating Parole 83

Bibliography 96
Index 98

CRIME, JUSTICE, AND PUNISHMENT

CAPITAL PUNISHMENT

CHILDREN, VIOLENCE, AND MURDER

CLASSIC CONS AND SWINDLES

CRIMES AGAINST CHILDREN:
CHILD ABUSE AND NEGLECT

CRIMES AGAINST HUMANITY

CRIMES AGAINST WOMEN

CYBER CRIMES

DEFENSE LAWYERS

DRUGS, CRIME,
AND CRIMINAL JUSTICE

THE DUTY TO RESCUE

ESPIONAGE AND TREASON

THE FBI

THE FBI'S MOST WANTED

FORENSIC SCIENCE

GANGS AND CRIME

THE GRAND JURY

GREAT PROSECUTIONS

GREAT ROBBERIES

GUNS, CRIME, AND
THE SECOND AMENDMENT

HATE CRIMES

HIGH CRIMES AND MISDEMEANORS:
THE IMPEACHMENT PROCESS

INFAMOUS TRIALS

THE INSANITY DEFENSE

JUDGES AND SENTENCING

THE JURY SYSTEM

JUVENILE CRIME

MAJOR UNSOLVED CRIMES

ORGANIZED CRIME

POLICE AND POLICING

PRISONS

PRIVATE INVESTIGATORS
AND BOUNTY HUNTERS

PROBATION AND PAROLE

PUNISHMENT AND REHABILITATION

RACE, CRIME, AND PUNISHMENT

REVENGE AND RETRIBUTION

RIGHTS OF THE ACCUSED

SERIAL MURDER

TERRORISM

VICTIMLESS CRIMES

VICTIMS AND VICTIMS' RIGHTS

WHITE-COLLAR CRIME

Fears and Fascinations:

An Introduction to Crime, Justice, and Punishment

By Austin Sarat

We live with crime and images of crime all around us. Crime evokes in most of us a deep aversion, a feeling of profound vulnerability, but it also evokes an equally deep fascination. Today, in major American cities the fear of crime is a major fact of life, some would say a disproportionate response to the realities of crime. Yet the fear of crime is real, palpable in the quickened steps and furtive glances of people walking down darkened streets. At the same time, we eagerly follow crime stories on television and in movies. We watch with a "who done it" curiosity, eager to see the illicit deed done, the investigation undertaken, the miscreant brought to justice and given his just deserts. On the streets the presence of crime is a reminder of our own vulnerability and the precariousness of our taken-for-granted rights and freedoms. On television and in the movies the crime story gives us a chance to probe our own darker motives, to ask "Is there a criminal within?" as well as to feel the collective satisfaction of seeing justice done.

Fear and fascination, these two poles of our engagement with crime, are, of course, only part of the story. Crime is, after all, a major social and legal problem, not just an issue of our individual psychology. Politicians today use our fear of, and fascination with, crime for political advantage. How we respond to crime, as well as to the political uses of the crime issue, tells us a lot about who we are as a people as well as what we value and what we tolerate. Is our response compassionate or severe? Do we seek to understand or to punish, to enact an angry vengeance or to rehabilitate and welcome the criminal back into our midst? The CRIME, JUSTICE, AND PUNISHMENT series is designed to explore these themes, to ask why we are fearful and fascinated, to probe the meanings and motivations of crimes and criminals and of our responses to them, and, finally, to ask what we can learn about ourselves and the society in which we live by examining our responses to crime.

Crime is always a challenge to the prevailing normative order and a test of the values and commitments of law-abiding people. It is sometimes a Raskolnikov-like act of defiance, an assertion of the unwillingness of some to live according to the rules of conduct laid out by organized society. In this sense, crime marks the limits of the law and reminds us of law's all-too-regular failures. Yet sometimes there is more desperation than defiance in criminal acts; sometimes they signal a deep pathology or need in the criminal. To confront crime is thus also to come face-to-face with the reality of social difference, of class privilege and extreme deprivation, of race and racism, of children neglected, abandoned, or abused whose response is to enact on others what they have experienced themselves. And occasionally crime, or what is labeled a criminal act, represents a call for justice, an appeal to a higher moral order against the inadequacies of existing law.

Figuring out the meaning of crime and the motivations of criminals and whether crime arises from defiance, desperation, or the appeal for justice is never an easy task. The motivations and meanings of crime are as varied as are the persons who engage in criminal conduct. They are as mysterious as any of the mysteries of the human soul. Yet the desire to know the secrets of crime and the criminal is a strong one, for in that knowledge may lie one step on the road to protection, if not an assurance of one's own personal safety. Nonetheless, as strong as that desire may be, there is no available technology that can allow us to know the whys of crime with much confidence, let alone a scientific certainty. We can, however, capture something about crime by studying the defiance, desperation, and quest for justice that may be associated with it. Books in the CRIME, JUSTICE, AND PUNISHMENT series will take up that challenge. They tell stories of crime and criminals, some famous, most not, some glamorous and exciting, most mundane and commonplace.

This series will, in addition, take a sober look at American criminal justice, at the procedures through which we investigate crimes and identify criminals, at the institutions in which innocence or guilt is determined. In these procedures and institutions we confront the thrill of the chase as well as the challenge of protecting the rights of those who defy our laws. It is through the efficiency and dedication of law enforcement that we might capture the criminal; it is in the rare instances of their corruption or brutality that we feel perhaps our deepest betrayal. Police, prosecutors, defense lawyers, judges, and jurors administer criminal justice and in their daily actions give substance to the guarantees of the Bill of Rights. What is an adversarial system of justice? How does it work? Why do we have it? Books in the CRIME, JUSTICE, AND PUNISHMENT series will examine the thrill of the chase as we seek to capture the criminal. They will also reveal the drama and majesty of the criminal trial as well as the day-to-day reality of a criminal justice system in which trials are the exception and negotiated pleas of guilty are the rule.

When the trial is over or the plea has been entered, when we have separated the innocent from the guilty, the moment of punishment has arrived. The injunction to punish the guilty, to respond to pain inflicted by inflicting pain, is as old as civilization itself. "An eye for an eye and a tooth for a tooth" is a biblical reminder that punishment must measure pain for pain. But our response to the criminal must be better than and different from the crime itself. The biblical admonition, along with the constitutional prohibition of "cruel and unusual punishment," signals that we seek to punish justly and to be just not only in the determination of who can and should be punished, but in how we punish as well. But neither reminder tells us what to do with the wrongdoer. Do we rape the rapist, or burn the home of the arsonist? Surely justice and decency say no. But, if not, then how can and should we punish? In a world in which punishment is neither identical to the crime nor an automatic response to it, choices must be made and we must make them. Books in the CRIME, JUSTICE, AND PUNISHMENT series will examine those choices and the practices, and politics, of punishment. How do we punish and why do we punish as we do? What can we learn about the rationality and appropriateness of today's responses to crime by examining our past and its responses? What works? Is there, and can there be, a just measure of pain?

CRIME, JUSTICE, AND PUNISHMENT brings together books on some of the great themes of human social life. The books in this series capture our fear and fascination with crime and examine our responses to it. They remind us of the deadly seriousness of these subjects. They bring together themes in law, literature, and popular culture to challenge us to think again, to think anew, about subjects that go to the heart of who we are and how we can and will live together.

*   *   *   *   *

Throughout the 1990s and into the new century, Americans have demanded that the government "get tough" on crime. Policies emphasizing treatment and rehabilitation of offenders were displaced by more punitive, more restrictive responses. We seem no longer to believe that criminals can be brought back into the "mainstream." As a result, we seem to want protection. We want those convicted of committing criminal offenses removed from society, incapacitated, and hopefully deterred. Among the most important casualties of these desires have been our practices of probation, diverting persons from prison, and parole, allowing early release from prison.

In this well-written, lively, and comprehensive book, Richard Worth combines cases and vivid examples to document the role probation and parole have played in the American criminal justice system. He shows how probation and parole were used in constructing sentencing systems that gave maximum leeway to officials to use the promise of no or released jail time in their dealings with offenders. This system encountered its most devastating setback in the presidential campaign of 1988, in which a horrible crime committed by a convict on a prison furlough—Willie Horton—became the symbol of a system gone astray.

Among the important issues examined in this timely and penetrating book are the questions of whether one philosophy of punishment should be applied to all kinds of prisoners, and whether we are a better society if we respond to crime with hope or with a fearful vengeance. By addressing these questions, *Probation and Parole* reminds us that who is punished and how says as much about those who do the punishing as about those who are punished.

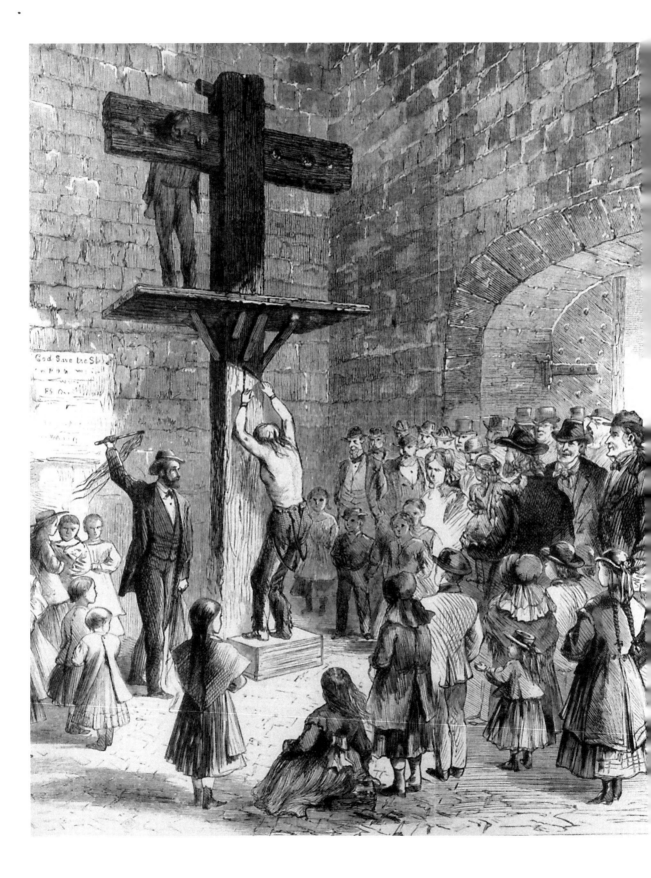

COPING WITH CRIMINALS: A BRIEF HISTORY

In the fall of 1988, the face of a convicted murderer named Willie Horton flashed across television screens in millions of American homes from coast to coast. Overnight, Horton became a veritable media celebrity. And in the November elections he helped George Bush become president of the United States. How had a criminal like Horton come to play such a key role in a presidential election? The answer says a great deal about America's criminal justice system, especially how it deals with important issues like parole or probation.

Fourteen years earlier, on October 26, 1974, Horton and two accomplices held up a gas station in Lawrence, Massachusetts. The thieves stole $250 and stabbed the attendant 19 times, killing him. The three men were soon arrested. The following April they went on trial, and after listening to the evidence, the jury deliberated only a short time before finding all three defendants guilty of murder and armed robbery. The judge sentenced them to life in prison without parole.

At age 23, Horton found himself locked behind bars at a maximum-security prison in Walpole, Massachusetts. Over the next few years, however, he became a model prisoner, and eventually the authorities moved him to the Northeast Correctional Center, a minimum-security prison for inmates who were nonviolent and not likely to escape. Horton also participated in community service programs, doing volunteer work at a state mental health center. These programs were usually reserved for prisoners expected to get parole. But prison authorities also believed that such programs had a place even where "lifers" like Horton were concerned: offering these convicts rewards, such as the opportunity to leave prison and work in the community, made them more manageable for prison personnel.

These same prisoners were also offered furloughs, so they could go home for a day and visit their families. Again, although furloughs were usually reserved for prisoners expected to be granted parole in the near future, many lifers would eventually have their sentences shortened and be released from prison. Community work programs and furloughs would help pave the way for these prisoners to resume normal lives again upon release by keeping them in touch with friends and family. Indeed, Horton took advantage of furloughs in 1985 and 1986 to visit his little girl. Of course, furloughs for convicted murderers, especially those who couldn't look forward to parole, involved risks. They might try to escape. They might even commit other violent crimes while outside the prison walls. But in Massachusetts, the risk was considered acceptable because only about 3 percent of the lifers had ever escaped.

In June 1986, Horton became one of the 3 percent, escaping while he was on furlough. It was later established that he had traveled to New York and later Florida. Willie Horton reappeared on April 3, 1987, when he broke into the house of Angela Miller and Cliff Barnes in Maryland. When Barnes came home from work that evening, he was confronted by a masked man with a gun who took his wallet. The man tied Barnes up in the basement. A few hours later, when Miller arrived home, she was surprised by a man wearing pantyhose over his head and pointing a gun at her. Horton demanded Miller's bank card so he could withdraw the money in her checking account. He found the card in her purse, then he began taking off the jewelry she was wearing. After he finished, Horton raped her.

Meanwhile, Barnes had escaped from the basement and run to a nearby house for help. After he called 911, the police arrived and chased Horton, who had gotten away in a car. Following a brief shoot-out, the police finally captured the furlough escapee, who had been on the run for about 10 months. Late that fall, Horton stood trial and was sentenced to life in prison for raping Miller.

This might have been the end of the story. While these events were occurring, however, the Democratic governor of Massachusetts, Michael Dukakis, was preparing to run for president. The press in Massachusetts took hold of the story about Horton and demanded to know why convicted murderers were allowed to go home on furloughs. Meanwhile, a citizens' group began forming that called on the state legislature and the governor to change the furlough policy. Dukakis, who had supported this policy—as had his Republican predecessor—finally agreed that furloughs for lifers must end.

But the Republicans refused to let the story die. They believed that crime would be a major issue in the 1988 presidential campaign. Polls showed that many Americans wanted tougher laws to deal with

During the 1988 presidential campaign, the case of Willie Horton, a murderer who escaped during a prison furlough and later committed a rape, damaged the chances of Democratic nominee Michael Dukakis—and cast attention on America's probation and parole systems.

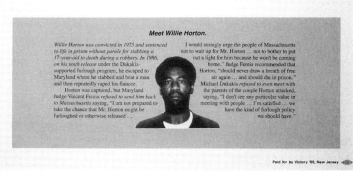

Gov 'gave pardons to 21 drug dealers'

Will Dukakis Turn Gun Owners Into Criminals... While Murderers Go Free?

The Most Soft-on-Crime Governor in Massachusetts History Is a Leading Advocate of Gun Control

Gun Owner Magazine quotes Dukakis as saying in 1986, **"I don't believe in people owning guns, only the police and military. And I'm going to do everything I can to disarm this state."** In 1976 Dukakis supported a (losing) statewide referendum which would have done just that. Dukakis has called for **federal registration** of all concealable handguns and has written, "... the solution to the problem of gun-inflicted violence must come at the national level."

Michael Dukakis talks about fighting crime, but there is a big gap between the *rhetoric* and the *record*. Maybe that's why the **Boston Police Patrolmen's Association unanimously endorsed George Bush for President.**

While trying to deny the citizens of Massachusetts the right to defend themselves, Dukakis has put more convicted criminals on the streets than any governor in his state's history.

• He has used his gubernatorial pardoning power to commute the sentences of *44 convicted murderers*—a record for the state of Massachusetts.

• He has vetoed and continues to oppose the death penalty *under any circumstances*, even for cop-killers, drug kingpins and traitors.

• He *opposes* mandatory sentences for hardcore criminals but *supports* mandatory sentences for anyone caught with an unregistered gun *of any kind*.

Dukakis has also presided over and actively endorsed the *most liberal prisoner furlough program in America*, **the only one in the nation** releasing prisoners sentenced to life without parole.

• On average, in the state of Massachusetts, one convicted first degree murderer was released *every day* over the last seven years.

• Since the beginning of Dukakis' second term as Governor, 1,905 furloughs have been granted to first degree murderers and at least 4,459 furloughs to second degree murderers. He has given 2,565 furloughs to drug offenders.

• In 1986 alone, Dukakis gave 1,229 furloughs to sex crime offenders, including 220 to persons charged with *six or more* sex offenses.

• Today 85 **violent felons from Massachusetts are on the loose** in America—set free on furloughs, they never bothered to come back.

Meet Willie Horton.

Willie Horton was convicted in 1975 and sentenced to life in prison without parole for stabbing a 17-year-old to death during a robbery. In 1986, on his tenth release under the Dukakis-supported furlough program, he escaped to Maryland where he stabbed and beat a man and then repeatedly raped his fiancee.

Horton was captured, but Maryland Judge Vincent Femia *refused to send him back to Massachusetts* saying, "I am not prepared to take the chance that Mr. Horton might be furloughed or otherwise released . . .

I would strongly urge the people of Massachusetts not to wait up for Mr. Horton ... not to bother to put out a light for him because he won't be coming home." Judge Femia recommended that Horton, "should never draw a breath of free air again ... and should die in prison." Michael Dukakis *refused to even meet* with the parents of the couple Horton attacked, saying, "I don't see any particular value in meeting with people ... I'm satisfied ... we have the kind of furlough policy we should have."

Paid for by Victory '88, New Jersey

criminals and reduce the high rate of crime. Strategists for George Bush, the Republican presidential nominee, began running advertisements that talked about murderers who were not eligible for parole committing crimes while temporarily out of prison. One of these commercials featured Willie Horton. It ended with the words: "Weekend prison passes. Dukakis on crime." The strategy proved successful. Dukakis, who had been leading Bush, gradually began to lose ground. In November, Bush was elected president—in large part, political observers concluded, because he had demanded a tougher approach to dealing with criminals like Willie Horton.

Getting tough with criminals is nothing new. For centuries, leaders have believed that the best way to deal with people who commit crimes is to mete out harsh punishments. As long ago as the 18th century B.C., under the Babylonian ruler Hammurabi, a code of law was written down that included heavy penalties for criminals. Although the social status of the offender made a difference, Hammurabi's approach was essentially an "eye for an eye"—offenders were to be punished with an equal measure of pain as they had caused. During the 7th century B.C., a political leader in Athens named Draco developed an equally harsh approach to handing out justice—even for people who committed only minor offenses. Draco called for thieves to be hanged and liars to have their tongues removed. To this day, the term *draconian* means harsh or cruel.

During the Middle Ages, suspected criminals were routinely tortured to obtain confessions, then they were hanged or their heads were chopped off. In England, even relatively minor offenses, such as stealing, were punishable by death. Some criminals were fortunate enough to escape this fate by being sent to the English colonies.

In the 18th century, the English philanthropist James Oglethorpe, for example, planned to settle Georgia with debtors. In England failure to pay debts routinely led to imprisonment, often for long periods and sometimes with one's entire family. Given this prospect, immigrating to the harsh American wilderness seemed like a better option for many debtors.

During the colonial period in America, convicted criminals commonly faced what would today be considered barbaric physical punishments. In

Richmond, Virginia, for example, a whipping post stood next to the courthouse. Once a person was found guilty, he or she would immediately be tied there and whipped. In 1773 a man convicted of stealing from a local shop in Connecticut was branded on the forehead. Branding criminals was not uncommon. In the minds of colonial Americans, it served at least three purposes: to inflict immediate physical pain on an offender, to stigmatize the offender for the rest of his or her life, and to enable law-abiding citizens to see easily who among them couldn't be trusted.

Less barbaric, but designed similarly to humiliate those who broke the law, were the pillory, a wooden frame that restrained an offender's head and hands, and the stocks, a wooden frame that restrained the feet or the feet and hands. The town pillories or stocks would be placed in a public place, where a lawbreaker's neighbors could insult—or even throw garbage at—him or her for the day or two the offender was thus confined.

For the most serious offenses, authorities turned to capital punishment, and the preferred method for carrying it out was hanging. Hangings were public events that generally drew large crowds of men, women, and even children. In addition to permitting law-abiding citizens to see retribution taken against the criminal, a public hanging was believed to serve as a deterrent to other would-be lawbreakers.

Conspicuously absent from the array of punishments meted out to criminals in colonial America was imprisonment. Physical structures didn't exist for the incarceration of large numbers of lawbreakers, but more importantly, the philosophical underpinnings of incarceration as a response to crime hadn't been explored. Punishment for lawbreakers was immediate, and its goal was first and foremost to exact revenge upon the criminal in the name of society.

Hanging was the primary means of dealing with serious criminals during the colonial period in America.

By the middle of the 18th century, however, some thinkers had begun to question accepted methods of dealing with criminals. In 1764 Cesare Beccaria, an Italian lawyer, published *On Crimes and Punishments*. Beccaria's book not only called for an end to torture and to the death penalty, but also advocated a fundamental shift in the way governments approached crime. Rather than simply taking revenge on criminals, Beccaria suggested, governments should do everything in their power to prevent crime in the first place. For those who had already broken the law, Beccaria advocated the use of prisons, where, removed from society, criminals would have the opportunity to reform themselves.

The ideas of Beccaria and other reformers gradually took hold in the United States after the Revolutionary War. America's Founding Fathers enshrined in the Constitution the right of every citizen to be free from "cruel and unusual punishments," regardless of what crimes the citizen may have committed. And within three years of the Constitution's ratification, Philadelphia had begun an experiment that would forever change the way wrongdoers were treated—not only in the United States but in the whole world.

Inspired by the city's nonviolent Quakers, in 1790 Philadelphia opened the first prison in the United States. Prison officials believed that criminals weren't evil but were simply wayward souls who had lost their moral way. The goal of the prison sentence, therefore, was to help the criminal recognize the error of his conduct (the facility initially confined only men) and then to reform. Prisoners were always kept in solitary confinement, and—to prevent even minimal contact with others—they were blindfolded whenever prison officials had to move them around the facility. Their only reading material was the Bible. Removing all other distractions, it was thought, would force the criminal to contemplate his crimes, and he would eventually repent and want to reform. (This philosophy led to use of the term *penitentiary* as a synonym for *prison*, for convicts at these institutions were supposed to be penitent, or sorry, for their crimes.) After prison officials believed that the convict had begun to repent, they would give him tools and materials to work at a trade in his cell.

The Philadelphia system, as the approach pioneered in the City of Brotherly Love came to be called, gained supporters throughout western Europe. Reformers from various countries visited Philadelphia, returned to their homelands, and set up similar penitentiaries there. But the Philadelphia system had a major drawback: expense. Because prisoners spent all their time alone in their cells—eating, sleeping, and working—the cells had to be rather large. This meant that to accommodate an inmate population of any substantial size, a Philadelphia-style penitentiary had to be huge, which in turn involved high construction costs.

In 1816 a prison opened in Auburn, New York, that would prove much more cost-effective. The mission of this penitentiary remained the same as its predecessor in Philadelphia: to reform inmates. But the physical layout and the entire prison experience here were radically different. Instead of large cells designed to house a single prisoner each, this prison had large cell blocks that contained many small cells. That was possible because the prisoners only slept in their cells. In a departure from the Philadelphia system, officials at the Auburn prison didn't keep prisoners perpetually in solitary confinement. Although they weren't allowed to talk with one another, convicts ate meals together in a large cafeteria, and they worked together in large shops. The sizable pool of free labor made the prison very cost-effective, and largely because of this the Auburn system, as it came to be called, gradually replaced the Philadelphia system. Its philosophy also continued to diverge from the spirit that had earlier motivated Philadelphia's gentle Quakers. Advocates of the Auburn system believed in treating their inmates harshly because they felt that a criminal's spirit had to be broken before reform was possible.

Meanwhile, a somewhat different approach to reform was being practiced by Captain Alexander Maconochie in Australia. For many years, British criminals had been transported to Australia, a crown possession. Those who committed new crimes, however, landed in brutal prisons such as one on Norfolk Island off the Australian coast. When Maconochie became head of the Norfolk Island prison, he decided that harsh punishments weren't the best way to transform criminals into upstanding members of society. Maconochie introduced the so-called mark system, whereby prisoners who behaved themselves could earn points, or marks, that would shorten their sentences. By contrast, misbehavior would lead to the loss of marks and would lengthen a sentence. As a convict's sentence approached its end, Maconochie gave him more freedom and imposed less supervision. This, he believed, would help prepare the inmate for his return to society. "The convict shall be punished for the past," Maconochie said, "and trained for the future."

A similar system was used in Ireland during the 19th century, with prisoners rewarded for good behavior by being allowed to work on community projects outside the prison walls. If they found paying jobs, the prisoners were eventually released before their sentences ended, although they continued to be supervised by the authorities. This practice, called the "ticket to leave," was the beginning of the modern parole system. (Parole today refers to any arrangement whereby a prisoner is released before the

The Australian penal colony on Norfolk Island. Here Alexander Maconochie pioneered the mark system, by which inmates could earn time off their sentences through good behavior.

end of his or her sentence and returned to the community under some type of supervision.)

Parole seemed a practical yet compassionate way to reward prisoners who had turned their lives around. But during the 1800s at least one man believed that not all criminals needed to go to prison to reform themselves. In 1841 John Augustus, a successful boot maker who lived in Boston, happened to be in court when a man was dragged before the judge for drunkenness—an offense usually punished by a jail sentence. Augustus intervened, declaring that he would put up bail for the drunkard if he agreed to sign a pledge to remain sober. Augustus also required that the man eventually return to court and show the judge that he had stopped drinking. Over the next 18 years, Augustus helped an estimated 2,000 people who had committed small offenses stay out of jail. He screened every man and woman carefully to make sure they were good candidates for reform before deciding to help them. "Great care was observed of course to ascertain whether the prisoners were promising subjects for probation," Augustus said, "and to this end it was necessary to take into consideration the previous character of the person."

Augustus appears to be the first person to use the term *probation* in the modern penological sense: allowing an offender to stay in the community under some supervision without going to jail. At first, the boot maker took lawbreakers to live in his home, but eventually he set up a special institution to house them. During the 1870s, Boston became the first city in America to have a probation officer to supervise criminals, allowing them to remain in the community instead of being put behind bars.

As the 19th century progressed, prison authorities seemed to lose sight of the original goal of penitentiaries—to reform inmates—and instead permitted horrible living conditions and the routine use of brutal punishments. In 1870 the National Congress of Penitentiary and Reformatory Discipline was formed in Cincinnati, Ohio, to change the treatment of criminals. Attendees called for an improvement in prison conditions so that prisoners could be reformed rather than simply punished. The congress also

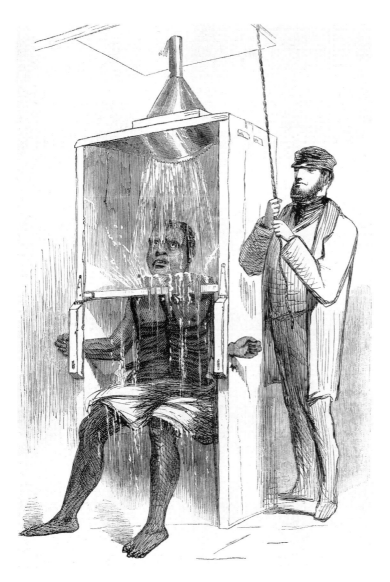

Throughout the 19th century, prison officials routinely tortured inmates. By 1870 the National Congress of Penitentiary and Reformatory Discipline called for an end to such practices so that prisoners could be reformed rather than simply punished. The congress also advocated the use of parole for rehabilitated inmates.

supported the use of parole based on the mark system pioneered in Australia.

These reforms were put into practice a few years later at the Elmira State Reformatory in northern New York, whose inmate population consisted mainly of young criminals who had been put behind bars after their first offense. Led by Zebulon Brockway, the administration at Elmira relied on education, job

Inmates at the Elmira State Reformatory in New York listen to a lecture in the prison auditorium. Officials at Elmira used education and job training to prepare prisoners for an early return to society through parole.

training, and parole to transform these criminals and help them return to society as soon as possible.

Unfortunately, few other prisons adopted Elmira's approach. This was a period when notorious thieves like Jesse James and the Dalton gang were holding up banks, robbing trains, and murdering innocent people. The general attitude of most Americans was that criminals posed a serious threat and should be locked away for as long as possible and severely punished for their crimes. No amount of education or job training, most people felt, could transform a hardened criminal into a good citizen who belonged back in society. Prison wardens generally agreed.

By the end of the 19th century, however, a new approach to the treatment of criminals had begun to develop as part of a general reform movement that was sweeping across America. Reformers began linking unjust social conditions to crime. In the slums of the nation's growing cities, for example, the poor lived crammed together in rundown tenement buildings. Men, women, and even young children were forced to toil long hours in dangerous factories, risking their health and their lives for extremely low wages. As journalists called muckrakers exposed these conditions, many middle-class Americans began to see the need for social change. They also were receptive to new theories that explained crime as an outgrowth of poverty and injustice.

By the early years of the 20th century, criminals were no longer seen as simply evil people but as individuals whose lives had been shaped by their families and their community—forces over which they had no control. Criminal behavior was viewed as an illness that could be cured, but only under the right conditions.

As a result, conditions inside prisons began to change. Prisons became correctional institutions where the emphasis was on helping prisoners learn how to deal with their psychological problems, correct the way they had been used to living, and return to society as law-abiding citizens. In effect, prison philosophy had come full circle: like the Philadelphia Quaker reformers of more than a century before, early-20th-century penologists wanted to rehabilitate rather than punish.

In keeping with this philosophy, parole came into wide use; offenders who had proven themselves ready to leave their cells permanently saw their sentences shortened. Probation also became the preferred option for dealing with many criminals who had committed less serious offenses—especially young, first-time offenders. Experts believed these people could accomplish far more by staying out of prison and remaining in the community. A variety of programs were established that provided young offenders with counseling, assisted them in dealing with drug problems, and gave them educational opportunities and job training.

The trend toward giving criminals help rather than simply punishing them continued through the 1960s. By the late 1970s, however, crime rates were increasing and public opinion began to shift. Many Americans now wanted lawbreakers punished severely, and they weren't particularly interested in whether those lawbreakers had grown up poor or disadvantaged. Politicians responded. Some declared that America's justice system coddled criminals and maintained that this was at least partly to blame for rising crime rates. Declaring oneself "tough on crime" became a winning political tactic.

In the last two decades of the 20th century, members of Congress and state legislators enacted a series of laws designed to punish criminals more harshly. These included laws requiring that persons convicted of certain offenses receive no less than a specified prison sentence, and that they serve the full amount of the specified minimum before being eligible for parole. These mandatory minimum sentences applied particularly to violent and repeat felons; a number of states even passed so-called three-strikes laws, which required judges to impose life imprisonment with no chance of parole for a third (usually violent) felony conviction. But even certain nonviolent criminals, particularly drug offenders, fell under mandatory minimum sentencing laws. In part as a result of these trends, the number of people incarcerated in America's prisons and jails has more than tripled since 1980, reaching 2 million by 2001. And almost 85 percent of these prisoners are nonviolent offenders. While granting parole and probation may not necessarily be in keeping with the get-tough-on-criminals approach most Americans still seem to favor, the high cost of housing and feeding so many prisoners virtually ensures that these two practices will continue to be used.

PROBATION

woman is caught trying to steal a blouse and a turtleneck shirt from a clothing store. Arrested and convicted of shoplifting, she has her sentence suspended and is given two years' probation instead of being put behind bars. A professional football player pleads guilty to possessing illegal drugs. But instead of going to prison, he is required to spend 1,000 hours working as a volunteer at a drug rehabilitation center as part of his probation.

Today, probation is increasing rapidly as a method of handling people who commit crimes. With the total prison and jail population at about 2 million, more than 3 million adults are on probation. Of the adults

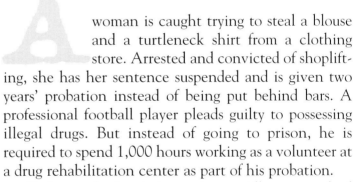

Baltimore Ravens linebacker Ray Lewis answers questions at a press conference after pleading guilty to obstruction of justice for hindering a police murder investigation in Atlanta. Lewis, like hundreds of thousands of first-time offenders each year, received probation.

who receive probation, more than 20 percent are women, and their numbers have been growing over the past two decades.

Those most commonly offered probation are first-time offenders whose crimes are considered relatively minor, such as shoplifters, drunk drivers who haven't injured or killed anyone, and people charged with possession of small amounts of some illegal drugs. After the defendant enters a guilty plea or is convicted at trial, the judge suspends his or her sentence and allows the offender to remain in the community under certain conditions.

Probation is offered for a variety of philosophical and practical reasons. First of all, society reserves harsher punishments for more serious criminals; not everyone who breaks the law deserves to lose his or her freedom. Even if, for example, we accept the fact that a drug abuser needs to change his or her behavior, that may be more easily accomplished if the person remains in the community than if he or she is sent to prison. Correctional institutions contain violent criminals who prey on first-time offenders, particularly when they are young. Placing someone who poses little or no risk to society in the midst of hardened criminals is not only unfair, it's also unlikely to lead the person to reform himself or herself. On the contrary, many experts believe, a prison sentence tends to transform many lesser offenders into habitual—and often violent—criminals.

By contrast, an offender who avoids prison and remains in the community can benefit from the support derived from unbroken relationships with friends and family. The chance to hold a job and earn a salary may also promote responsibility and socially acceptable behavior.

As a practical matter, probation is also far less expensive—about 90 percent less expensive—than putting a criminal behind bars. Some experts estimate

the average annual cost of keeping a person in prison—including food, health care, guards, and other expenses—at about $25,000. Building new prisons to accommodate the growing ranks of inmates adds significantly to that total. Plus, when a person is behind bars, the government loses the chance to collect from her or him income and payroll taxes.

Beginning in the late 19th century, when Massachusetts first provided probation for criminals throughout the state, probation services spread across the country. By 1967 every state offered them. Probation officers have always played a key role in the entire process. For example, they prepare a presentence investigation (PSI), which helps a judge determine whether to grant probation. The PSI includes factual information such as

Arrested on drug charges, this 17-year-old was given probation and ordered to attend academic classes to earn her high school diploma. Offenders who avoid prison terms generally have much better chances for success in society.

a description of the crime and the offender's past criminal record, educational background, family relationships, and employment. In addition, the report contains the probation officer's recommendation as to whether the offender should be incarcerated or be given probation.

If an offender is given probation, it's a probation officer's job to make sure that the offender doesn't violate the terms of his or her probation agreement. Such violations—which can lead to a prison sentence—include, of course, the commission of another crime. But a person on probation is also expected to stay drug-free, not to leave the area without permission from the probation officer, and not to change addresses without informing the officer. While probation is far less restrictive than being inside a prison, it isn't supposed to give an offender the same freedom as a law-abiding citizen receives. And the probation may be immediately ended if any terms of the agreement are broken.

Many probation officers, however, see their jobs as far more than making sure offenders observe the letter of the probation rules. They also try to help the offenders under their supervision improve their lives. This often involves directing them toward community services, drug counseling, job training, and educational programs. Linda Tabb, a probation specialist in Florida, encourages clients to view their situation as an opportunity. "I always try to tell them it's a base for learning to do things better than what you were doing," she says. "A lot of people in the public don't know it, but people [on probation] do turn their lives around."

Criminal justice professionals recognize that not all offenders on probation are alike. Offenders are classified according to the threat they pose to the community and the types of services they need to turn their lives around. Those who regularly abused drugs or committed a previous crime fall into the high-risk category and may require more than standard probation. In their cases, probation may be combined with another form of punishment, called an intermediate sanction. This is a penalty stronger than probation, but not as strong as being placed behind bars.

A mild sanction may be a fine, the amount depending on the offender's salary and the seriousness of his or her crime. Imposing a fine, it is believed, may add enough bite to probation to persuade an offender not to break the law again. Fines might be imposed for vandalism, for example, or for issuing a check when there is no money in the bank to cover it.

Judges may also require criminals who receive probation to make restitution to their victims. A youth who smashed the windows of a neighbor's car might, for example, have to reimburse the neighbor for the cost of replacing the windows.

Probation is frequently combined with community service as well. This might entail picking up trash along highways, rivers, or seashores; working in hospitals, drug-rehabilitation centers, or schools; or painting over graffiti. The use of unpaid community service as a way of dealing with lawbreakers dates to the mid-1960s, when a California judge handed out that sentence to a group of women who had run up large traffic fines but had no money with which to pay them.

Community service combined with minimal supervision may be appropriate for many offenders on probation, but others require more restrictive treatment. One approach frequently used with higher-risk offenders is called intensive supervision. Under an intensive-supervision program, the probation officer's caseload is dramatically reduced—enabling him or her to monitor each offender much more closely than would be possible with a typically large caseload. Probation officers in intensive-supervision programs can meet regularly with each client, see that the offender is receiving necessary treatment or counseling, make sure that community

Former Olympic figure skater Tonya Harding trims grass at a cemetery as part of the community service requirement of her probation; Harding had been charged with disorderly conduct. Community service for probationers was pioneered in California in the 1960s.

service is being completed, and ensure that all of the terms of the probation are being fulfilled. Intensive supervision also typically requires that an offender submit to frequent drug tests and observe strict curfews, staying at home during specified hours.

Sometimes intensive-supervision programs use electronic monitoring, whereby a special bracelet that sends out a signal is placed around the offender's wrist or ankle. This enables probation officials to keep track of an offender's whereabouts at all times. If, for example, an offender isn't at home during his or her mandated curfew, the probation officer will soon find out and can quickly take action. Electronic monitoring can work in two ways. In the first method, the bracelet can send out a regular signal to a receiver in the offender's home telephone. This signal is then transmitted over the phone lines to a computer that is monitored by probation officers. If the signal stops, it means the offender is no longer near the telephone and has violated the curfew. In the second type of electronic monitoring, a computer periodically calls the offender's telephone number. The offender must put the bracelet in a box connected to the telephone to show that he or she is still there. A video camera placed by the box prevents the offender from giving the bracelet to someone else and leaving home.

The careful monitoring that characterizes intensive supervision is also a feature of day-reporting centers. Approximately half the states use this alternative to prison, which requires offenders to call in regularly throughout the day. In Massachusetts, for example, an offender must meet with a member of the center staff each day to work out a schedule of activities for the next day. After the day's events, offenders must go to the center to participate in various programs, such as drug abuse counseling, high school courses, and assistance in finding a steady job. Participants are also checked at their homes in the evening to make sure they have not gone out. As time goes on and offenders demonstrate that they are willing to live by the rules, they may be given less and less supervision.

PAROLE

Pete Rose was one of the greatest baseball players in history. Nicknamed "Charlie Hustle" because he always seemed to give his all—whether at the plate, on the base paths, or in the field—Rose collected more base hits than any other player in history. He won three National League batting titles and played on World Series championship teams at Cincinnati and Philadelphia. After retiring as a player, Rose became the manager of the Cincinnati Reds, a team for which he had played for 15 years.

In the late 1980s, however, Rose ran afoul of major league baseball officials when it came to light that he had been betting on baseball games—a practice prohibited in the wake of the 1919 Black Sox scandal. Rose was banned from the game he loved, but that didn't end his troubles. The gambling revelations led to a government investigation of the baseball star's finances, and that investigation turned up evidence

Crime victims watch, via a video screen, a parole board hearing at Pelican Bay Prison in California. Though it isn't particularly popular with the public, parole continues to be widely used.

39

Major league baseball's all-time hit leader, Pete Rose, also became one of America's most famous parolees.

that Rose had avoided paying income tax on all his earnings. He received a jail sentence but after serving a few months was released on parole and ordered to do community service.

While Pete Rose may be one of America's most famous parolees, his experience is shared by hundreds of thousands of others who are released before their sentences are up. The word *parole* comes from a French term meaning "word of honor." Initially it referred to prisoners of war who were released by their enemies if they promised not to go back into battle again. During the American colonial period, a type of parole existed in England whereby prisoners were released and shipped to the colonies to become indentured servants until their sentences had been completed. These indentured servants worked on farms and tobacco plantations for their masters.

During the 19th century a form of parole called the "ticket to leave" was introduced in Ireland. In the Irish capital of Dublin, parolees were expected to report regularly to an Inspector of Released Prisoners, who also helped them find jobs.

The first American parole system began during the last part of the 19th century at the Elmira Reformatory in upstate New York. Elmira's forward-thinking superintendent, Zebulon Brockway, and his staff rewarded inmates for reforming their lives with increasing amounts of freedom until they were finally released on parole. The decision to parole a prisoner was based on his good conduct at the reformatory, his participation in education and job training programs, and his prospects for finding employment outside the penitentiary. Once a parolee left Elmira, he was expected to check in once a month with a member of the reformatory staff.

Parole gradually became available to inmates at other prison facilities across the United States, and by 1922 almost every state operated a parole system. Parole went hand in hand with a practice known as indeterminate sentencing. Under indeterminate sentencing, a convict entering prison didn't know the precise length of time he or she would be spending behind bars. When the offender received the sentence, the judge would announce a minimum amount of time he or she must serve as well as a maximum amount of time. Within these limits, the actual length of the sentence was determined by the inmate's behavior in prison. For example, the inmate could earn "good time," whereby prison authorities would give the prisoner one day off his or her sentence for every day he or she demonstrated good conduct in prison. In this way, prisoners could substantially reduce the length of time they spent behind bars, and prison staffs benefited because inmates were much more likely to be cooperative.

Decisions on whether to grant parole are made by state parole boards, which regularly review a prisoner's performance and determine whether she or he is eligible for early release. Appointed by the governor, a parole board may consist of corrections professionals as well as people from other walks of life. Members of the board hold hearings at which they review a report on each prisoner before deciding whether he or she should receive parole. These reports are prepared by parole officers, who provide vital information on the prisoner, such as the offense for which he or she is currently serving time, previous crimes or prison sentences, and previous history of drug abuse, if any. The report also details the progress the inmate has made in prison, including days of good conduct and training programs or psychological counseling attended.

From this information, the parole board must decide whether releasing the inmate back into the community constitutes an acceptable risk to public safety. Sometimes parole is denied because board members are concerned, after looking at the report, that the inmate might commit another crime. Sometimes they reject the parole application because they believe that the inmate should remain involved in some type of treatment program inside prison before being released. The board may also decide to put off a decision until obtaining further information, or it may decide to grant parole.

Some experts have criticized parole boards, saying that many of their members don't have experience in the field of criminal justice or that hearings are much too short to consider all the relevant information on

an inmate. Plus, critics point to instances in which parole boards made the "wrong" decision—and there are many such cases—releasing a prisoner who proceeded to commit a serious, generally violent crime. As a result of these criticisms—and as part of the public's more general call to get tough on criminals—some states have eliminated parole boards entirely. Others have greatly reduced the authority of the boards to decide whether a prisoner should be released.

In addition, state legislatures have passed laws that require tougher sentences for criminals committing

A young offender takes a moment to collect his thoughts while being questioned by parole board members. Parole boards are charged with the difficult task of determining whether specific prisoners can safely be released into society before the completion of their sentences.

Prison overcrowding and cost are two compelling reasons for the use of parole.

plan. Such a plan may include where they will work and live, what treatment they will receive, and whether they should enroll in job training and educational courses. Parole officers also discuss the guidelines offenders must follow once they are released. These are similar to the conditions that apply to probation. For example, the parole officer must be informed if an individual changes her or his address, decides to leave the state, or starts a new job. The parolee is also not permitted to use drugs, carry a weapon, associate with criminals, and, most important, commit another crime.

As an inmate is being considered for parole, the parole officer may help him or her enter various kinds of release programs. One of these is called a furlough—the type of release that was granted to the infamous Willie Horton. Unlike in Horton's case, however, furloughs are generally granted only to prisoners who are almost ready to complete their sentences. An inmate on furlough is allowed to leave prison usually for a period of about one to three days. The inmate may use this time to make necessary arrangements for his or her postrelease life—for example, by finding a place to live or applying for a job. Furloughs also enable prisoners to visit with their families and strengthen ties with friends in the community. After the furlough has ended, the prisoner is required to return to his or her cell.

Another type of program, called work release, allows inmates to work in the community during the day. They must, however, return to the correctional center at night. At one program, for example, the center staff works closely with inmates to set up job interviews and provide transportation to a job site. Each inmate is expected to hand over part of his or her earnings to the center to pay for room and board. Parolees also handle chores, such as cleaning, in the correctional center and can enroll in drug therapy sessions as well as a program run by Alcoholics Anonymous to help them overcome drinking problems. Inmates usually spend about 30 to 45 days in the program before being released into the community under the supervision of a parole officer.

Many communities have halfway houses where people on parole or probation can live if they are not yet deemed ready for independent lives. Pete Rose, for example, spent three months at a halfway house in Cincinnati, about the average amount of time parolees spend in these facilities. Halfway houses were first established in Massachusetts in 1817. Different types of offenders might be assigned to halfway houses, including those who have committed robbery, crimes involving drugs, and in some cases even murder. In a halfway house program, parolees leave during the day to go to their jobs, but return to the facility in the evening. They are usually assigned a variety of chores, including cleaning, cooking, lawn mowing, and gardening. While nationwide more than 35,000 halfway houses are in operation, some communities have been reluctant to accept them. Neighbors are often fearful of having released prisoners living near them, believing that the ex-cons might pose a risk to their or their family's safety.

Sometimes a criminal is sentenced to a short period in jail (typically 30 to 120 days) to get an experience of what it's like to be behind bars, then released to a facility called a boot camp. Pioneered by Georgia and Oklahoma during the 1980s, boot camps have spread to a majority of the states. The early boot camps were just for men, but camps have also been set up for women. These facilities are designed primarily for young offenders who, it is hoped, can be dissuaded from a career in crime by a stay of about six months in a rigorous, demanding, military-like environment. Boot camps are similar to basic training in the armed forces. As one expert put it, their purpose "is to break the prisoners down, strip them of their street identity, and then . . . build them up by providing discipline and self-control."

Offenders get up early in the morning and march

out to a parade ground. As they march, they might sing a song, like this one:

> Warden, warden can't you see
> What this program's done for me.
> Sat me down in a barber chair
> Turned around and had no hair.
> Took away my faded jeans
> Now I'm wearing army greens.

As soon as prisoners enter a boot camp, they are treated like raw recruits in the armed forces. Their hair is cut short, and they are issued special uniforms. Many hours each day are spent in marching, drills, and exercise. All the while, supervisors bark orders at the inmates like drill sergeants in the army. At one

A parolee in his room at a halfway house in Ogden, Utah. Halfway houses, where the typical stay is about three months, are designed to help convicts make the transition back into free society.

Inmates at the Sumter County Correctional Institution boot camp, Bushnell, Florida. Boot camps, which are used especially with young offenders, are designed to instill self-discipline and respect for authority.

facility, an officer yells to the inmates: "Are you motivated?" The inmates are expected to shout back: "Motivated! Motivated! Motivated! Sir!" Parolees march to breakfast and afterward march in formation to work areas where they usually do community service projects. Following dinner, they participate in programs that include academic courses and psychological counseling. Ideally, boot camps teach self-discipline and self-respect while introducing parolees to a new lifestyle that doesn't involve crime.

But boot camps also exist simply because they help

reduce overcrowding in prisons and save money. Although boot camps may initially be more expensive because they have more staff and special programs than prisons, parolees spend less time in boot camp, so in the long run the cost may be less. Unfortunately, some parolees find the harsh discipline at boot camp so difficult that they try to escape or ask to be returned to prison. After about six months, parolees who complete the boot camp program are released into the community, but they are carefully monitored by parole officers.

One of the major responsibilities of parole officers is to supervise released criminals to make sure they don't violate the guidelines of their parole or commit new crimes. "Impulsiveness is a hallmark of criminal behavior," says Colorado parole officer James Saint John. "You're dealing with people who already have broken the rules repeatedly." Monitoring parolees has become more and more difficult, however, because parole officers often handle huge caseloads. While 30 to 50 parolees may be the ideal number for a parole officer, most supervise many more than that. In Colorado, for example, the average caseload is up to 80, making it very difficult for parole officers to adequately monitor all the activities of the people under their supervision. Many parole officers also function as probation officers as well.

Instead of substantially increasing the number of parole officers, however, most states have been spending their money on building more prisons. Nevertheless, it's far cheaper to place an offender on parole than to keep him or her in prison. The average cost of keeping a criminal behind bars is approximately $25,000, whereas the average parolee costs a state less than 10 percent that amount. Overcrowding in prisons has also meant that many serious offenders are being let out on parole. Among parolees, about 25 percent have been convicted of violent crimes such as murder or assault, while more than a third have been involved in serious property offenses such as car theft and burglary.

"When you're handling caseloads like this, you have to prioritize," said one official who trains parole officers. "You have to focus on your high-risk offenders, and juggle things. And you hope it doesn't backfire." Parole officers are expected to monitor offenders regularly, checking with an employer to find out if they show up for work, calling or visiting their homes to make sure they haven't moved, and requiring them to report in frequently (especially the high-risk offenders).

Some of these parolees require very tight monitoring. Several years ago, Maryland began offering inmates a chance to be released on parole if they agreed to enter another, more strictly supervised program. They could choose from boot camp, house arrest, day reporting, and intensive supervision—much like people on probation. Parolees under house arrest are required to wear an electronic device on their ankles and told that if they leave their homes without permission, the ankle bracelet will send out a signal that they have violated parole. Offenders must also submit to regular drug tests, and if there is evidence of drug use, they are required to go into a therapy program.

In some states inmates are released from prison and placed under intensive supervision. After the experience of being behind bars, criminals often find that the chance to go back into the community, even under intensive supervision, is a much more pleasant alternative. Parole officers involved in this program have a much smaller caseload so they can monitor offenders more closely. Parolees are expected to hold jobs and do community service work. Under this type of program, many parolees decide to change their lives. As one parole officer put it: "It's great when I get clients who decide they truly want to turn their lives around. It feels good to know I might have had some positive influence on them and their future." Despite what the public may believe, many offenders do complete their paroles successfully.

The actual time a person spends on parole varies with the type of offense. Usually offenders spend about 40 percent of their sentences on parole and the rest of the time behind bars. Unfortunately, some offenders violate their parole guidelines. Perhaps they are caught using drugs, or carrying a weapon, or moving out of state without telling their parole officers. Other parolees may be arrested and charged with committing a new crime. When these problems occur, parolees receive court hearings to determine whether they are guilty of violating their parole. If so, parole may be ended, and they are returned to prison.

Juvenile Crime: Probation and Aftercare

On May 20, 1999, a 15-year-old named T. J. Solomon walked into Heritage High School in Conyers, Georgia, and shot six students with a .22-caliber rifle. All six of the wounded students recovered. Solomon, an accomplished marksman, apparently aimed low, according to some reports because he didn't want to kill anyone. Nevertheless, after hearings in juvenile court, Judge William Schneider ruled that Solomon should be tried as an adult—even though 18 is the usual age of adulthood under the law.

Eventually Solomon entered a plea of guilty but mentally ill—there was evidence that he suffered from bipolar disorder—to nine counts of aggravated assault and five weapons counts. On November 10, 2000, a superior court judge in Rockdale County, Georgia,

The Los Angeles County Probation Department trains young offenders to fight forest fires. Forestry, conservation, and wilderness camps are used as alternatives to incarceration for some juvenile delinquents.

T. J. Solomon, 15 when he wounded six students in a school shooting spree, received a 40-year prison sentence. Increasingly, violent juveniles like Solomon are ending up in adult criminal courts.

sentenced the boy to two consecutive 20-year sentences. Later the Georgia State Board of Pardons and Paroles, following its standard policy, established a tentative parole month of May 2035. Solomon will serve a minimum of 36 years, or 90 percent of the sentence handed down by the superior court judge. A teenager at the time of the shooting, he'll emerge from prison a middle-aged man in his fifties.

Had he committed his crime 30 years earlier, the

outcome for T. J. Solomon would probably have been quite different. Juvenile offenders were very rarely tried as adults; the overwhelming majority of cases went through the juvenile justice system. And in the juvenile justice system, incarceration, when ordered, would last only until the offender reached his or her 18th (or in some jurisdictions, 21st) birthday. At that time, regardless of the offense, the offender would be released—and records of the case would be sealed.

As the case of T. J. Solomon indicates, however, times have changed. More and more state legislatures have passed laws designed to get tough with young offenders. In Wisconsin, for example, kids as young as 10 can be tried in adult criminal court for murder. In Oregon, 15-year-olds who commit violent crimes can be tried as adults and given stiff sentences. Florida prosecutes as adults several thousand serious juvenile offenders each year. The Sunshine State also puts more youths in prison than any other state.

States began dealing with juvenile offenders this way in the late 1970s and early 1980s, in the face of rising rates of violent crime committed by young people. Even when the murder rate among adults began declining between 1987 and 1993, the number of youths arrested for homicide more than doubled.

Since then, however, violent juvenile crime—like adult crime—has declined. Through the 1990s the juvenile homicide rate fell by 40 percent, and other violent offenses by juveniles, such as rape, robbery, and aggravated assault, also dropped.

Still, almost 3 million youths under the age of 18 are arrested each year. Many of these arrests are for so-called status offenses, such as running away from home, purchasing alcohol, or truancy (failing to go to school). These are considered violations only because of the status of the offender, who is under the age of adulthood. But other young people commit offenses that would be considered crimes regardless of the age of the offender.

In spite of this, youths who commit crimes aren't referred to as criminals but as delinquents—individuals not in accord with accepted behavior or the law. Although the distinction is largely semantic, it nevertheless reflects a long tradition of viewing juvenile offenders as essentially different from their adult counterparts, and for this reason according them special treatment.

The first juvenile court system was established in 1899 in Chicago. Over the next two decades, the idea spread throughout the country. From the beginning, the basic premise of the juvenile justice system has been that young offenders must be treated differently from adults who break the law. First of all, it is widely accepted that children—having limited experience and ability to reason—aren't as responsible for their own behavior as are adults. In addition, because they are still developing morally and intellectually, children are generally thought to be more responsive to treatment. In other words, compared with an average adult offender, it's more likely that an average young offender can be reformed.

Thus the rules and procedures used in the juvenile justice system diverge from those used in the adult criminal justice system. In the adult criminal justice system, jury trials are held to determine the guilt or innocence of the defendant. Those trials are adversarial proceedings, with lawyers for the defendant arguing against prosecutors (the lawyers for the state) and the judge acting as a referee. In juvenile court, by contrast, proceedings aren't even called trials but rather adjudication hearings. The judge rather than a jury determines the facts of the case, and the proceedings are closed to the public. If the judge decides that the juvenile has committed an offense, the juvenile is not said have been convicted of a crime but to have been adjudicated delinquent. And instead of being sentenced, the juvenile is said to receive a disposition.

Juvenile delinquents at Dobbs-Ferry-on-Hudson, New York, work in the kitchen at their facility, 1938. The juvenile justice system, which began in 1899, is based on the belief that young offenders are essentially different from adult criminals and require special treatment.

Again, these differences may seem largely semantic, but they are all designed to avoid stigmatizing the juvenile as a criminal.

In theory, everyone involved in the juvenile justice system—from the judge, to the lawyers, to the probation officers and social workers—has the same goal: to do what is in the best interests of the offender. Punishing wrongdoing takes a backseat to reforming the wrongdoer.

By far the most common disposition that juveniles receive is probation. Juvenile probation began in the early 20th century, and by 1918 juvenile probation officers had been appointed throughout the country. The majority of juveniles on probation have committed property offenses such as burglary and auto theft. But some have violated drug laws or been involved in violent crimes. Like probation officers who supervise adult criminals, many probation officers who deal with juvenile offenders have huge caseloads, making it almost impossible for them to provide adequate supervision and counseling for the juveniles assigned to them. This makes it more likely that a higher proportion of the young offenders will get into further trouble with the law.

To deal with this problem, cities like Boston have tried to strengthen the juvenile probation system. Boston has started a program called Operation Nite Lite, which is aimed at preventing serious juvenile offenders from violating the terms of their probation. As part of the program, police and probation officers travel together in squad cars during the evenings. Since probation officers are unarmed, Operation Nite Lite now enables them to go safely into the most dangerous sections of the city to check on their clients. A probation officer knocks on the door, interviews the juvenile to ensure that he or she is keeping curfew, and talks with parents or guardians to find out whether the youth has been behaving. Patrol cars might also stop at a street corner where a group of young people is gathered to find out if a probationer is among them.

"Feedback from offenders, police, parents, and community members alike indicate that the kids are aware that things have changed," wrote Ronald P. Corbett Jr. and Bernard L. Fitzgerald of the Massachusetts probation department, "and [they] have become more cautious, not to say compliant, in their behavior. This is a breakthrough." Law enforcement officials in Boston estimate that more than 20 percent of all serious crime is committed by probationers, so a program like

Operation Nite Lite can be extremely effective. Indeed, the murder rate among young people in the city has plummeted, and many experts give Operation Nite Lite part of the credit.

Parents, too, seem to recognize that keeping teenagers at home can help protect them from falling victim to violent crime. While the increased surveillance by police and probation officers has helped deter crime, other programs have also been introduced to improve the lives of young people in Boston. Police officials have established a summer jobs program, a camp for kids, and even basketball leagues. And community centers provide drug treatment and counseling for young people looking for alternatives to gangs.

In southern Minnesota a different type of program targets young people with emotional problems who have committed violent crimes. "Probably 80 percent of the kids have been arrested and are on probation," says Tom Adkins, a corrections official. Counselors meet with youthful offenders, their parents, and other relatives to develop an individualized program that will provide effective treatment. At the beginning, a therapist may conduct counseling sessions with the juvenile delinquent several times each week. The counselors also try to coordinate other community services that may be helpful, such as drug therapy, recreation programs, and summer camps. Unlike Operation Nite Lite, this program focuses far more on treatment. It is the last opportunity some offenders have before they are placed in a detention facility.

Many juvenile programs often work with low-risk offenders. Some of these juveniles never appear in court. Instead, police officers may feel that their case is not serious enough to require a hearing, and they are immediately ordered onto probation. Juveniles may also be required to make restitution for their offenses and work on community service projects. "We're moving the system from a counseling . . . approach to one that gives the offenders a far greater sense of accountability," explains Dennis Maloney, a justice official in Oregon. The program that he describes includes a special court where a youthful offender faces a jury of teenagers who decide what his or her penalty should be for committing an illegal act. "The kids come up with far more creative stuff than we ever would," Maloney says. "If you vandalize the school, you might not only have to clean the school, but you might also have to go to the student council and make a presentation about what . . . you were thinking when you did it."

Another element of the program involves mediation. An offender guilty of theft, for example, might have to sit across from her or his victim and a mediator. After hearing from the youth and the victim, the mediator would decide what the sentence should be—usually some kind of community service. Although most young people complete their sentences successfully and their cases are dismissed, those who don't may wind up in juvenile court. Thus, the program combines rewards and punishments.

Many areas require youths who are guilty of crimes such as shoplifting or check fraud to make restitution by paying back the amount that they stole from wages earned at a part-time job or a community service project. In Utah a large study examined more than 90,000 young people who had committed burglary, auto theft, or vandalism to find out whether making restitution had any impact on the rate at which they committed new crimes. The juvenile offenders either paid their victims back immediately or in installments from the money they earned by working on community service projects. It was hoped that by making restitution, the youths would develop a greater sense of responsibility and understand the seriousness of their crimes so that they would be less likely to break the law again. Among youths put on probation without going through the court system, the rate of repeat crimes for those paying restitution was only 11 percent, whereas the rate for those who didn't pay restitution was 18 percent. A similar gap was found among more serious offenders who went through the court system, though their overall rate of recidivism (committing new crimes) was higher. Those who had to pay restitution reoffended at a rate of 32 percent; those who didn't have to pay restitution, at a rate of 38 percent. Clearly restitution has an impact on the rate of repeat crimes.

The state of Maryland has instituted a restitution program called Earn It. The business community and local churches help youthful offenders find jobs, but in return juveniles are expected to make restitution payments out of the wages they earn. Another program puts probation officers in the schools to monitor youths on probation and ensure that they are attending classes. A third program includes volunteers from colleges and the community who serve as mentors for troubled youths and help them reform their lives. These services combine surveillance with accountability and rehabilitation.

For more serious offenders, Maryland provides day treatment programs—much like those for adults. While youths remain at home, they attend centers during the day that provide high school courses, counseling, and drug treatment. Electronic monitoring is also used with serious offenders who remain at home before coming up for a hearing, as well as with juvenile delinquents who are under intensive probation supervision.

About one-third of all juvenile courts rely on intensive supervision for juvenile delinquents. In one program in Ohio, youths remained in a detention center for five days, then spent the next two weeks under house arrest. During the following 10 days, the youths attended school and a drug treatment program, but the rest of the time they were expected to abide by strict curfews and had to ask permission from their counselors to leave home. Anyone who violated these guidelines was sent back to the detention center. The one-year recidivism rate for juveniles in this program was 40 percent.

Each year about 10 percent of the juvenile delinquents who receive court hearings are sent to correctional facilities. These centers date to the early 19th century, when New York started its House of Refuge for delinquent and neglected children. Similar reform centers opened in Boston and Philadelphia. Young people were required to wear uniforms and sleep in locked cells, and they received corporal punishments if they stepped out of line.

During the 1990s, more than 100,000 young people were placed in secure correctional facilities, such as detention centers and training schools, each year. Often the juvenile delinquents put behind bars are serious offenders who have committed multiple crimes. Such youths make up only about 15 percent of all juvenile offenders, but they account for about three-fourths of all violent crimes. As children, they often achieved failing grades in school and were constantly misbehaving in the classroom. They often joined gangs and began their criminal activities even before becoming teenagers, resulting in frequent encounters with the police and repeated arrests until they were eventually confined in a correctional institution.

Many of these juvenile facilities are overcrowded and have been severely criticized for providing very little treatment to help juvenile delinquents go back into the community and avoid a life of crime. Instead, critics charge, young people at these facilities run an unacceptably high risk of being sexually abused, and many develop into more serious criminals. Still, the worst juvenile facilities are probably preferable to the best adult prisons. And in 1996, more than 8,000 youthful offenders were being housed in state prisons for adults. Only about half of these youths were living in separate facilities; the rest remained with the adult inmates.

Some states have closed state training schools,

believing that they have a negative impact on youthful offenders. In Kentucky, for example, juvenile delinquents are now housed in small treatment facilities and group homes, where the youths live with a professional staff that provides counseling and supervision. Many states place serious offenders in forestry camps, ranches, and wilderness programs. These began during the 1930s, when delinquent boys were sent to camps and required to build roads and perform forestry work in national parks. Wilderness programs offer outdoor activities, such as mountain climbing and canoeing, designed to help youths build self-esteem, learn to trust

Members of the Crips gang, Los Angeles. Many high-risk juvenile offenders are gang members.

others, and develop teamwork. Some programs also help the poor through community service projects. It is hoped that young people can apply these same values once they leave the wilderness program and go back home, avoiding a return to crime.

Maryland, for example, runs a 16-week Youth Leadership Challenge Program, which emphasizes rigorous training that enforces the values of self-esteem, responsibility, and self-discipline. Once youths complete the program, they enter aftercare, which is similar to parole for adult offenders.

Aftercare is designed to provide a transition for young people from an institution to the community so they can return to school, find work, and avoid committing new crimes. In some cases, that transition may be supervised by an overworked probation officer with a heavy caseload who has very little time to spend with each youth. But some areas provide more intensive aftercare. In Kentucky, for example, juveniles attend a day treatment program that includes counseling, academic courses, career education, and assistance in finding a job. Some wilderness programs try to ensure that the skills young people developed in the woods are used once they return to the streets. In one such program, counselors saw that youthful offenders became involved in community service projects and found full-time employment once they returned to their homes.

In 1989 Michigan began the Nokomis Challenge Program to provide a wilderness experience for youthful offenders as an alternative to putting them in an institution. Those who entered the program were serious juvenile delinquents who had already been arrested several times and had committed violent crimes. They spent three months in the wilderness program and another nine months in aftercare, receiving therapy to change their values and improve their family relationships. While this program cost less than keeping delinquents in an institution, the rate of repeat crime was higher: almost twice as many youths in the Nokomis program committed new crimes. As the experts who studied the program concluded, "The intensive aftercare . . . must be strengthened to help prevent youth from [committing new offenses]."

Effective aftercare should enable young people to make the transition back into the community, whether they return to school or go to work. Because of the wide range of problems juvenile delinquents may have, a good aftercare program should offer a variety of services. These might include drug therapy; help in developing interpersonal skills, so the youths can interact effectively with their family and friends; and instruction in coping skills, to teach the offenders how to deal with anger and stress. Special education teachers are also generally needed, because many youthful offenders have below-average academic skills.

An aftercare program in Bradenton, Florida, for example, helps youths who are dealing with a drug problem. The youths live in a treatment center where they receive drug treatment as well as a variety of other services designed to teach them how to solve personal problems, find meaningful work, and pass their high school courses. Eventually, program participants return home, where they receive intensive supervision from a probation officer. Meanwhile, they continue to receive drug treatment and career training so they can hold down jobs. The Bradenton program combines rehabilitation and surveillance, as youths learn to take on greater responsibility for their own lives.

The purpose of any successful probation or aftercare program is to help youthful offenders transform themselves into law-abiding, productive members of society. States and cities use a variety of approaches that include restitution, intensive supervision, day treatment, and boot camps. These programs emphasize rehabilitation, monitoring, and accountability—all aimed at enabling young people to become successful adults.

5

DOES PROBATION WORK?

A young man named Gerry breaks into several homes in a wealthy suburb, stealing jewelry and electronic equipment. When he tries to sell some of the stolen items, he is arrested. Instead of receiving a prison sentence, Gerry, a first-time offender, is placed on probation. Three months after his probation begins, however, Gerry breaks into another home. This time he is surprised by the homeowner, panics, and shoots her before fleeing.

Every year we hear about stories like this one—in which the criminal justice system gives a lawbreaker a second chance, only to have him or her turn around and commit a more serious crime. The result

A police officer in Nashville, Tennessee, transports a repeat offender to her precinct to be processed. Many Americans take a dim view of probation because of the high percentage of probationers who commit further crimes.

is that public opinion favors giving probation to fewer felons—even first-time offenders—and putting more of them behind bars. As one congressman observed, "Anyone who is locked up will not commit a crime." By the turn of the 21st century, about 2 million Americans were behind bars. Indeed, the rate of incarceration in the United States, which more than tripled between 1980 and 1999, is currently the highest in the world.

Has the rising rate of incarceration affected crime rates? It's hard to say for sure, because many factors contribute to crime rates. However, from 1985 to 1991, as more felons were put behind bars, the crime rate continued to increase. Violent crimes, for example, rose by 36 percent, with murders increasing by 24 percent. But from 1991 to 1995, with incarceration rates continuing to climb, violent crime overall fell by 10 percent (murders dropped by 16 percent), and property crime declined by 11 percent. For the rest of the 1990s, property crimes continued to decline; the trend also held for violent crime, which reached its lowest levels since the 1960s.

But this decline has not continued everywhere. For example, in New York City as a whole, the number of murders began rising again, increasing more than 8 percent from mid-1998 to mid-1999; in Brooklyn, New York, the rise in the murder rate over that period was much higher: 25 percent.

Thus, what impact the incarceration rate has on crime rates is open to debate. Supporters of more and longer prison sentences argue that the get-tough approach has lowered crime rates, pointing to the reduction in crime since 1991. Opponents counter that during much of the time that America was putting more felons behind bars, crime was in fact increasing. A more significant factor in the drop in crime, they argue, was the strong economy. Indeed, many critics deny that increased incarceration has any deterrent effect—that is, they believe, criminals don't reconsider committing their crimes because they fear longer prison sentences if caught. Much violent crime, these critics correctly point out, is committed impulsively; much property crime is committed by drug addicts who need money to support their habits. Such people aren't likely to consider rationally the possible consequences of the illegal acts they are about to commit. Then, too, a potential lawbreaker in a more lucid state might ask whether it's actually likely he or she will get caught. The government estimates that nearly 90 percent of all serious felonies committed each year go unreported or unsolved. Under the circumstances, then, is it reasonable to believe that longer or tougher sentences will stop potential criminals?

Many proponents of tougher sentencing argue that this is the wrong question to ask. The issue, they say, is not so much potential criminals, but actual ones. Prison sentences may or may not deter people contemplating the commission of a crime, but they do incapacitate criminals who have already been caught. In other words, for as long as a felon is behind bars, he or she cannot commit further crimes against society. Thus, more extensive use of prison sentences, rather than of probation, appears to be called for.

The issue becomes even more clouded when one considers that, even with tougher recent statutes such as mandatory minimum sentences, the large majority of jail and prison inmates will eventually be released back into society. And then what happens? Statistics show that more than 60 percent are rearrested for new crimes within three years. Is this high recidivism rate a valid argument for limiting the use of probation—or, for that matter, parole—on the theory that most criminals will keep committing crimes unless they are behind bars? Such theoretical considerations collide with practical

Whether probation or incarceration is more effective at preventing crime has been rendered somewhat of a moot question. Overcrowding in America's prisons and jails makes probation a practical necessity.

ones in America's overcrowded prison system. A majority of states have received court orders to reduce prison overcrowding. This is a primary reason why so many first-time criminals have been—and probably will continue to be—given probation.

But how well does the practice of granting probation serve society? One of the best ways to evaluate the probation system is to compare the rate of recidivism among probationers with that of former inmates in the prison system. A study conducted in California revealed that about two-thirds of the felons placed on probation were rearrested after three years, with half of them being convicted for their offenses. This is about equal to the recidivism rate among criminals who went to prison and were eventually released on parole. Joan R. Petersilia, a criminal justice expert who conducted the study, admitted that the rate of repeat crime among felons on probation is very serious but pointed out that the average amount of money spent on supervising a probationer is only about $200 annually. "It is no wonder that recidivism rates are so high," she said. Petersilia added that more felons are being given probation and that "they are in need of more supervision, not less. But less is exactly what they have been getting over the past decade."

Patrick Langan, a staff member of the U.S. Department of Justice's Bureau of Justice Statistics, also points out that about half the probationers who are supposed to be going to drug counseling or paying restitution to their victims are not doing these things. Heavy caseloads prevent probation officers from adequately supervising offenders to ensure that they follow the guidelines of their probation.

Even with these problems, however, some studies show that recidivism among probationers is lower than among criminals released from prison, although the results of different studies vary dramatically. For example, reports on programs in Missouri and Kentucky showed that only 22 percent of probationers were rearrested after three years, while a larger study of 79,000 felons conducted by the Bureau of Justice Statistics revealed a recidivism rate twice as high, 43 percent. Such large differences may be explained by various factors. The types of offenders in the studies may differ—criminals with drug problems, for example, are more likely to commit new crimes. The criminal histories of the offenders in different studies may also vary. Criminals who began committing felonies when they were young teenagers are more likely to become repeat offenders. In addition, probation officers in one area may be doing a much better job at detecting offenses, leading to more arrests.

Supporters of probation argue that even if the recidivism rates are about the same, probation is preferable to incarceration for many offenders because of its considerably lower cost. Opponents, however, are quick to point out something else. A prisoner who spends time in prison and on parole commits, on average, 20 percent fewer new crimes during the same period as a probationer because of the time spent behind bars. This may be another compelling reason to enforce stiffer sentences for criminals. Nevertheless, former prisoners are much more likely than probationers to be involved in burglaries. The reason may be that the stigma of serving time in prison and being released as a parolee makes it far more difficult to get a job.

Probation isn't the only alternative to prison, however. Some offenders receive sanctions such as intensive supervision, house arrest, electronic monitoring, and community service. Criminal justice experts who support these types of sanctions point out that they can reduce overcrowding in prisons while also saving money and enabling judges to make the punishment more closely match the seriousness of a particular crime.

A large survey conducted by Joan Petersilia and her associates examined 14 intensive-supervision programs in states such as California, Washington, New Mexico, Iowa, and Texas. These programs are more expensive than regular probation because probation officers carry smaller caseloads, enabling them to more closely monitor each offender. As a result, intensive-supervision programs are expected to be more effective at preventing recidivism. The Petersilia study compared criminals in intensive supervision with offenders who had committed

Young offenders perform their community service—painting over graffiti.

similar crimes but were on regular probation. What the researchers found was perhaps a bit surprising: the recidivism rate was about the same—approximately 33 percent—for offenders in both types of programs.

Does this mean that intensive supervision and probation are equally effective at preventing recidivism? The experts weren't sure. Since offenders are watched far more carefully under intensive supervision, more crimes may have been detected, while many new offenses committed by criminals on regular probation may not have been discovered. Probation officers involved in intensive supervision also discovered far more technical violations by probationers—

for example, failing to keep curfews, leaving the state without informing the probation officer, or using drugs. Approximately 65 percent of the probationers under intensive supervision were caught committing technical violations, compared with only 38 percent on probation. However, as the researchers reported, offenders had "higher rates of technical violations because of the closer supervision given to those in the program." Many of these violations were related to the use of drugs, and the violators were often sent back to prison. Therefore, the intensive-supervision program didn't really reduce prison overcrowding, as many experts hoped. Intensive supervision does cost less than prison, however, so the state reaped some financial benefit from the program.

Researchers also discovered that offenders who participated in regular drug treatment programs were less likely to commit repeat crimes. Recidivism is especially high among people who commit crimes involving drugs. Therefore, drug treatment might be expected to help them. Another factor that seems important is holding a job. Probationers commit fewer new felonies if they are employed and earning an income, perhaps because there is far less reason for them to make money dishonestly. Offenders who live with their families and have the support of a spouse and children are also more likely to have a successful probation.

How does intensive supervision of probationers compare with parole? A New Jersey study found that about one-fourth of the probationers were arrested again; the rate was 35 percent for parolees. In addition, the intensive supervision program saved an estimated $7,000 per criminal.

Among probationers in an intensive supervision program in Wisconsin, only 5 percent went back to prison, compared with 29 percent who were in a regular probation program. And far fewer of the

probationers under intensive supervision were convicted of violent crimes.

Los Angeles police make a drug
sweep. Recidivism is especially
high among drug abusers.

However, offenders in this type of program are
likely to be caught committing many more technical violations than those on regular probation. A
study in Georgia, for example, showed that the
number of technical violations uncovered was
almost double, resulting in prison sentences for
many of the probationers.

Intensive supervision is used not only with adults,
but with juvenile offenders as well. One program in

Toledo, Ohio, was initiated because of overcrowding in juvenile institutions. The program, which included several phases, lasted a total of 180 days. During the first phase, the juveniles were kept under house arrest except when they attended school and worked on community service projects. In addition, counselors met with them at least twice a week and gave them one drug test. The offenders also attended sessions for psychological therapy, substance abuse treatment, and career education. During a later phase of the program, the juveniles were required to abide by curfews, and drug testing continued, but the number of face-to-face meetings with the counselors was reduced. In fact, at each successive phase of the program, the level of supervision declined.

The juvenile offenders were monitored for an additional 18 months after completion of the program to determine how their rates of recidivism compared with those of youths confined in an institution and then released. About half of those under intensive supervision committed a felony, about the same rate as those who had been in detention. However, wrote juvenile justice expert Richard Wiebush in describing the results of the program, the intensive supervision enabled youths to avoid the experience of being incarcerated, which disrupts "family and community ties" and may force young people to deal with "intimidation and assault" in an institution. Nevertheless, some critics of intensive supervision point out that while juvenile offenders are in institutions they cannot commit crimes. But this advantage is short-lived, because many of them return to crime after being released from detention.

Studies in Michigan and Ohio also compared juveniles under intensive supervision with inmates in a detention center. The rates of recidivism were exactly the same, but the intensive supervision program cost only about one-fourth or one-third as much as incarceration.

Intensive supervision has often been combined with electronic monitoring to enforce curfews and house arrest. Offenders wear an electronic bracelet that sends out a signal to indicate that they are at home. Young people sometimes have difficulty with electronic monitoring because they lack the discipline to maintain tight schedules that require them to be at home, in school, or on a job at regular hours. As a result, youthful offenders usually have a much higher rate of technical violations while under electronic monitoring than do adult criminals. In some programs, only 17 percent of the adults had violations, compared with 83 percent of the young offenders. In addition, more juveniles were arrested for committing new crimes.

The success rate for electronic monitoring seems to increase the longer offenders are required to remain in the program. Experts who studied electronic monitoring in Florida, California, Oregon, and Kentucky found that the failure rate was only about 5 percent for people in electronic monitoring for 120 days. By contrast, the rate for offenders involved in the program for only 30 days was 15 percent. But the highest rates of failure were still among young people—more than 30 percent.

Electronic monitoring for adults was far more successful. A program started in southern Mississippi, for instance, with criminals on probation who had committed technical violations—they didn't check in with their probation officers or show up for work on community service projects—also included probationers who continued to abuse drugs and alcohol. Darren Gowen, who helped run the program, reported, "With both types of violators, we quickly observed the incredible deterrent effect of the electronic ankle bracelet," which forced offenders to

House arrest with electronic monitoring is a frequently used alternative to incarceration for young offenders. A judge in South Carolina added a twist when the 15-year-old delinquent at the left of this photo came before him: he ordered her to be shackled to her mother every waking minute for six weeks.

keep to a daily schedule and arrive at home or work when they were supposed to be there. The program also involved youthful offenders. Gowen described one young man who frequently used cocaine, especially at night and on weekends when he spent time with his friends. By keeping him at home in the evenings (except when he attended drug counseling sessions) and supervising his activities with electronic monitoring, probation officers could work with him much more effectively and help him deal with his problems.

Another type of program that involves careful monitoring is offered by day-reporting centers. Throughout the country there are more than 100 of these centers, which require probationers to call in regularly during the day if they are at work, to attend counseling sessions, and to remain at home in the evenings. One program included serious offenders who had been convicted of a crime at least six times in the past. The recidivism rate of these criminals over a two-year period topped 60 percent. While high, this is about the same rate at which felons are rearrested after being released on parole. Once again, however, the programs at day-reporting centers are less expensive than incarceration.

EVALUATING PAROLE

Sadie Tedesco holds a picture of her son, officer Gary Tedesco of the Lodi, New Jersey, police department, at a rally in support of life sentences without parole for convicted murderers. Tedesco and another Lodi police officer were killed by a convict whose sentence was later commuted.

In New York City, Anthony Mosomillo, a highly respected police officer, tried to arrest a criminal named Jose Serrano on drug charges, a violation of his parole. Before Mosomillo could make the arrest, however, Serrano shot and killed him. "There was no reason for this," the mayor of New York said afterward. "The man who did this was on parole. He should not have been on parole."

In Savannah, Georgia, a man released from prison on parole after being arrested for attempted robbery was accused of the brutal murder of his girl-friend. Police said he broke away from the electronic monitoring device that was supposed to keep him under surveillance.

In Pontiac, Michigan, law enforcement officials protested the release of a convicted cop killer named Janice Love. After serving less than half of her 50-year sentence for murder, Love was paroled. "We are highly disappointed," one official declared. "It makes the life of an officer who is sworn to serve and protect less than important. There's anger. Many of us are disheartened with the system."

The same could probably be said about a significant number of ordinary citizens. Each year more than 400,000 adult criminals are released from incarceration and placed under the supervision of a parole officer, and when individuals in this group are arrested again—especially for violent crimes such as murder, assault, and rape—people wonder how the system serves law-abiding citizens. The numbers do paint a dismal picture: of the 400,000 criminals paroled every year, nearly 175,000 will be rearrested for new offenses within three years of their release.

Perhaps in response to the public's concerns, an increasing number of parolees are being sent back to prison for technical violations of their parole, such as using drugs, carrying a weapon, spending time with other felons, or not checking in regularly with their parole officer. It's perhaps not surprising that in the atmosphere of the times, many parole officers worry about making a mistake that will have tragic consequences. Thus, they are more concerned about supervising rather than rehabilitating their parolees, and they are continually on the lookout for any technical violation. One officer described his job as "trail 'em, nail 'em, and jail 'em."

By the late 1990s, approximately 22 percent of state prison inmates were behind bars because they had violated parole. This represented a more than fourfold increase from the rate during the 1970s (5 percent).

This "revolving door" in America's prison system is not the way parole is supposed to work. Parole isn't a right of prisoners; only those who appear rehabilitated are supposed to receive it. Before a prisoner is approved for release, a parole officer evaluates the likelihood that the offender will commit another crime. Among the factors considered are the presence of

a drug problem, the nature of past crimes, previous prison sentences, and the offender's age at the time of his or her first offense. Those whose criminal career began early, experts believe, constitute a greater risk.

Unfortunately, these factors yield only a rough indication of the risk involved in paroling a particular offender. No foolproof way to predict recidivism exists, and probably none ever will. Thus, some criminals may remain behind bars because they look like bad risks for parole, when actually they aren't.

Judging which prisoners eligible for parole are no longer a threat to society is fraught with difficulty. This parole violator, who held police at bay with a gun for about two hours, was clearly not a good risk.

On the other hand, offenders who seem like good risks and are paroled often prove otherwise. As one expert put it: "A parole board may know that of 100 offenders with a certain set of characteristics, 80 will probably succeed and 20 will fail on parole. But the board members do not know whether the man who is before them belongs with the 80 or the 20."

Some critics of the corrections system have tried to deal with this problem by calling for longer mandatory sentences. If prisoners are kept behind bars longer, the reasoning goes, at least they'll be off the streets and can't commit crimes while they're locked up. In Michigan, for example, a new law requires convicts to serve a minimum sentence without parole for crimes such as murder. This law would have kept Janice Love behind bars for 50 years instead of allowing her to be released after serving only 21 years of her sentence. Officials in other states support laws that would require serious felons to serve up to 90 percent of their sentences for crimes such as rape, robbery, and assault. Under current conditions, most serve far less.

Across America, prisoners seem to be spending a longer part of their sentences behind bars before being released. The average time behind bars during the late 1990s was more than 40 months, compared with just over 30 months in 1985. It has become more difficult to get parole or earn good time for an early release. Yet criminal justice experts such as Dr. James Bonta point out that longer terms behind bars aren't very effective as a method of battling crime and reducing recidivism.

What are law enforcement officials doing to reduce recidivism and make parole more successful? In Washington State, police officials have started working with parole/probation officers to catch offenders who might be committing technical violations or new felonies. If, for example, police spot a group of people hanging out in the empty parking lot of a shopping mall during the night, they obtain names and addresses, then immediately file a report. If any of the individuals is on parole, his or her name will show up in a computerized crime information data base. This information is then sent to the Department of Corrections, which can determine whether the parolee has violated his or her parole guidelines by breaking curfew. Reporting on the program, authors Terry Morgan and Stephen Marrs point out that it "sent a strong message to the offender population that they had better abide by the conditions of their release and not commit new crimes."

Curfews are often part of intensive-supervision programs, such as the one used with parolees in New Jersey. These offenders spend at least 60 days in prison so they can experience the harshness of life behind bars, which presumably makes them more eager to stay in the community and to have a successful parole. Parole officers meet with offenders almost daily, test them for drugs several times each month, and require that they work in community service projects. About 40 percent of the parolees returned to prison during the first year they were involved in the program, most for drug violations. But the recidivism rate is somewhat lower than it is for other parolees.

Another program took low-risk offenders and put them under intensive supervision after less than three months in prison. The parole officer has a caseload of only 20 parolees, compared with more than 70 in a regular parole program. Only 19 percent of those under intensive supervision were rearrested, compared with 40 percent in a regular parole program. The number of technical violations was much higher for parolees under intensive supervision, probably because they were being watched so much more closely than offenders in other parole programs.

Surveillance of their clients has become the top priority for many parole officers. The system being shown in this January 24, 2001, demonstration tracks parolees using Global Positioning Satellite technology.

About 42 percent of offenders had technical violations; the percentage was only half that for offenders on regular parole.

Perhaps unfortunately, recidivism—a measure of failure—is the primary way parole programs are evaluated. There are no studies showing how many parolees successfully went back to work, or forged healthy relationships with spouses or children, or became upstanding members of the community. Instead, criminal justice officials look only at the rate of repeat crimes and technical violations.

The rate of recidivism was carefully monitored

among parolees involved in a work-release program in the state of Washington. Less than 5 percent committed new crimes while they were involved in work release, which seemed to help them successfully reenter their communities. About half the participants were involved in technical violations, including possession of drugs, and many of them returned to prison. Among those who successfully completed the program, however, the recidivism rate was no lower than it had been among prisoners who had served out their sentences. Perhaps one reason was that work-release parolees were serious offenders, who had committed a large number of crimes and often suffered from severe drug problems. The cost for maintaining both types of offenders—in prison or in work release—was about the same. However, the work-release programs do reduce prison overcrowding.

Another type of program that has been evaluated carefully because it seems to hold the promise of reducing recidivism is boot camp. Adults and juvenile offenders as young as 12 have been assigned to boot camps. After graduating from boot camp, the juveniles are sent to an aftercare program and receive intensive supervision. One study, conducted by the National Institute of Justice, looked at programs in Cleveland, Ohio; Denver, Colorado; and Mobile, Alabama. Up to 94 percent of participants successfully completed the programs, which not only helped them academically but also improved their self-discipline and physical health. Aftercare included high school courses as well as therapy aimed at ending drug use. Once the young people entered aftercare, however, problems began to develop. At most, only 50 percent graduated, and in one program the dropout rate was 7 in 10. One-fifth of the young people in Mobile were arrested for new crimes, while approximately one-third were rearrested in Cleveland and Denver.

Boot camps for adults were evaluated in eight states: Florida, Georgia, Illinois, Louisiana, New York, Oklahoma, South Carolina, and Texas. The rates of recidivism for participants in these programs were about the same as they were for other parolees. In New York, Louisiana, and Illinois, however, rearrests for new crimes seemed somewhat lower, perhaps because these states also had a six-month intensive-supervision program that followed boot camp. The New York program included many hours of physical exercise and training as well as an equal amount of time devoted to therapy for drug dependency. Some participants regarded the therapy as the crucial element. As one participant put it: "I would like to thank you for a second chance in life. The reason I say life is because if I had sat in prison I would have either wound up dead, or just rotted and my mind and body would have gone to waste worse than it was when I was abusing alcohol. . . . I have also become responsible for myself."

New York officials also estimated that the program saved the state about $20,000 per participant because it freed up space for other offenders in prison, avoiding the cost of building new correctional facilities. Recidivism rates were also better. Only 30 percent of the people who graduated from boot camp returned to prison after two years, whereas 36 percent of those who had been in prison and were released on parole went behind bars again. The program in New York, however, was far more successful than the boot camps in Arizona, where only a small number of offenders graduated. Boot camps also didn't save money in Arizona, and the state decided to end them in 1996.

In an even larger survey, the National Institute of Justice looked at more than 50 boot camps attended by juvenile offenders. In general, the rate of recidivism for those who graduated was about the same as for inmates placed on regular parole. But those who

Boot camp may work better if followed by an aftercare program.

graduated committed fewer total crimes than individuals who dropped out of the training. Only about one in four of the boot camps in the study had aftercare programs designed especially for graduates. Most people leaving boot camp went directly to intensive supervision, which emphasized surveillance instead of the counseling, therapy, and educational programs found in effective aftercare. As a result, the benefits of boot camp may have been lost.

Criminal justice experts who look at the results of programs with parolees realize that control and surveillance alone will not reduce recidivism. Studies of day-reporting centers, for example, show that up to half of the participants are returned to prison. And programs such as intensive supervision, boot camps, and work release do little better than regular parole in cutting down the number of rearrests. Only when these programs are combined with treatment and rehabilitation are the rates of recidivism improved. Treatment can be especially helpful when it is aimed at high-risk offenders who have committed serious crimes. Successful rehabilitation programs help change an offender's attitudes toward holding down a full-time job, dealing with authority, and using drugs.

In programs like these, recidivism is reduced on average 10 percent, but the most effective efforts aimed at parolees have achieved even better results—a 40 percent reduction in recidivism. These programs, which last from three to nine months, are focused primarily on treatment, not supervision. Therapists are carefully selected for a treatment style that meshes well with the needs of parolees. In addition, the therapists and the program as a whole are regularly evaluated for effectiveness. Instead of simply punishing offenders who step out of line, the treatment also tries to reward participants who make progress.

In one program, developed in Newfoundland, Canada, electronic monitoring was combined with therapy and drug abuse treatment for parolees. The parolees included serious, high-risk offenders as well as lower-risk criminals. All participants wore ankle bracelets to verify that they were abiding by the curfews that were an element of their house arrest.

More than 85 percent of the parolees completed the program without committing any new crimes or violations of the parole guidelines. When electronic monitoring alone had been used with these types of offenders, recidivism rates after the completion of the program were the same as for participants in a regular parole program—more than 50 percent. Results were different, however, when parolees were given a treatment program that included substance abuse therapy, anger management, and job training. For high-risk offenders who received this treatment, the

Perry Bernard, assistant director of Project Return, helps a parolee learn computer skills. Graduates of the New Orleans–based project have a recidivism rate of about 25 percent—half the statewide average in Louisiana —demonstrating that successful programs must offer alternatives to a life of crime.

recidivism rate was only about 30 percent. "Continued support of treatment programs for higher risk offenders," wrote James Bonta and his associates, "perhaps married with EM [electronic monitoring] to increase treatment attendance, is suggested."

Treatment programs aren't the only way to deal with the problem of recidivism for parolees. If fewer crimes are committed, then a smaller number of criminals would be sent to prison. In a recent report issued by the RAND Corporation, experts looked at the most cost-effective methods of reducing crimes. They estimated that $1 million spent on giving cash rewards to students so they would graduate from high school would prevent 258 crimes each year, while the same amount of money spent on parenting programs to help adults raise their children more effectively would eliminate 160 crimes each year. By contrast, building new prisons, the RAND report estimated, would prevent only 60 crimes annually. Clearly, prevention programs should at least be investigated as an approach to dealing with the crime problem.

Since crime is not likely to be entirely prevented any time in the near future, however, probation and parole will continue to be key elements in America's criminal justice system. In fact, the number of proba-tioners and parolees has recently topped 4 million. One of the problems with probation and parole, however, is a relatively high rate of recidivism. Some critics of the justice system have even argued that stiffer sentencing instead of probation, and longer sentences without the possibility of parole, would reduce the crime rate by keeping criminals behind bars so they can't commit offenses. Unfortunately, many criminals are involved in new crimes after they return to the community. As an alternative, law enforcement officials have designed a continuum of programs to deal with criminals— alternatives that lie between probation or parole on one end and prison on the other end. These alternatives involve strengthening the probation/parole system by using such measures as community service, intensive supervision, electronic monitoring, day-reporting centers, and boot camps. None of these approaches has achieved astounding success. Imperfect though they are, however, probation and parole will probably always be a necessary response to the intractable problem of crime.

Bibliography

Abadinsky, Howard. *Probation and Parole: Theory and Practice.* Englewood Cliffs, N.J.: Prentice Hall, 1991.

Abramsky, Sasha. "When They Get Out." *The Atlantic,* June 1999.

America's Prisons: Opposing Viewpoints. San Diego: Greenhaven Press, 1997.

Anderson, David. *Crime & the Politics of Hysteria: How the Willie Horton Story Changed American Justice.* New York: Times Books, 1995.

Bonta, James; Jennifer Rooney; and Suzanne Wallace-Capretta. "Electronic Monitoring in Canada." Public Works and Government Services Canada, 1999. Internet site: *http://www.sgc.gc.ca.*

Byrne, James; Arthur Lurigio; and Joan Petersilia, eds. *Smart Sentencing: The Emergence of Intermediate Sanctions.* Newbury Park, Calif.: Sage, 1992.

Carlson, Norman, et al. *Corrections in the 21st Century.* Belmont, Calif.: Wadsworth Publishing, 1999.

Clayton, Susan. "Young Probation/Parole Officer Toughens with Experience." *Corrections Today,* June 1996.

DiIulio, John. "Reinventing Parole and Probation." *Brookings Review,* Spring 1997.

Donziger, Steven, ed. *The Real War on Crime: The Report of the National Criminal Justice Commission.* New York: HarperCollins, 1996.

Dooley, Mike. "Restorative Juvenile Justice." *Corrections Today,* December 1997.

Durham, Alexis. *Crisis and Reform: Current Issues in American Punishment.* Boston: Little Brown, 1994.

Friedman, Lawrence. *Crime and Punishment in American History.* New York: Basic Books, 1993.

Harry, Jennifer. "Helping Turn Lives Around." *Corrections Today,* June 1998.

Jacobs, Nancy; Mark Siegel; and Jacquelyn Quiram, eds. *Prisons and Jails: A Deterrent to Crime?* Wylie, Tex.: Information Plus, 1997.

Jensen, Gary, and Dean Rojek. *Delinquency and Youth Crime*. Prospect Heights, Ill.: Waveland Press, 1992.

Lloyd, Jillian. "So Many Parolees, So Little Time." *Christian Science Monitor*, January 12, 1999.

Marcus, Jon. "Cleaning up Crime in Boston." *Scholastic Update*, November 2, 1998.

McClear, James. "Pontiac Cop Killer's Parole Protested." *Detroit News*, November 15, 1998.

McShane, Marilyn, and Wesley Krause. *Community Corrections*. New York: Macmillan, 1993.

Petersilia, Joan, ed. *Community Corrections: Probation, Parole and Intermediate Sanctions*. New York: Oxford University Press, 1998.

Petersilia, Joan, and Susan Turner. *Evaluating Intensive Supervision Probation/Parole: Results of a Nationwide Experiment*. National Institute of Justice, May 1993.

Rojek, Dean, and Gary Jensen. *Exploring Delinquency: Causes and Control*. Los Angeles: Roxbury Publishing, 1996.

Salzer, James. "Parole Board—Do the Crime, Serve the Time." *Savannah Morning News*, December 10, 1997.

Smykla, John Ortiz, and William L. Slelke, eds. *Intermediate Sanctions: Sentencing in the 1990s*. Cincinnati, Ohio: Anderson Publishing, 1995.

Wade, Beth. "Keeping Kids out of Court." *American City & County*, May 1998.

Wiebush, Richard. "Juvenile Intensive Supervision: The Impact on Felony Offenders Diverted from Institutional Placement." *Crime & Delinquency*, January 1993.

Index

Adjudication hearings, 58
Aftercare
    and boot camp, 89, 92
    and juvenile probation,
        66-67
Alabama, boot camp in, 89
Arizona, boot camp in, 90
Athens, punishments in, 17
Auburn system, 21-22
Augustus, John, 24
Australia, history of prisons
    in, 22, 25

Babylonia, punishments in,
    17
Barnes, Cliff, 15
Beccaria, Cesare, 20
Boot camps, 48-51, 89-92
Branding, 18
Brockway, Zebulon, 25-26,
    41
Bush, George, 13-17

California, probation in,
    72-73, 74, 79
Canada, parole in, 92-94
Capital punishment, 18
Colonial period
    parole in, 40-41
    punishments in, 17-18
Colorado, boot camp in, 89
Community service, 14,
    35-36, 61-62
Confessions, 17
Constitution, and prisons,
    20
Correctional facilities, 64-66
Curfews, 87

Dalton gang, 26

Day-reporting centers, 37,
    80-81, 92
Day treatment programs,
    63, 66
Delinquents, 58-59
    See also Juvenile justice
        system
Determinate sentences,
    43-44
Disposition, 58
Draco, 17
Drug offenders, 32, 44, 45
Drug treatment, 76
Dukakis, Michael, 15, 16-17

Earn It, 63
Electronic monitoring,
    36-37, 63, 79-80, 92-93
Elmira State Reformatory,
    25-26, 41
Employment, with proba-
    tion, 76
England, history of punish-
    ment in, 17
"Eye for an eye," 17

Family, and probation, 76
Federal sentencing guide-
    lines, 44
Fines, with probation, 35
Florida
    boot camp in, 90
    juvenile probation in,
        67, 79
Forestry camps, 65
Furloughs, 14-17, 47

Georgia, boot camp in, 90
Gowen, Darren, 79-80
Greece, punishments in, 17

Group homes, 65

Halfway houses, 48
Hammurabi, 17
Hangings, 18
Horton, Willie, 13-17, 47

Illinois
    boot camp in, 90
    first juvenile court in, 58
Indentured servants, 41
Indeterminate sentencing,
    41-42
Intensive supervision, 35-
    37, 52-53, 63-64, 74-78,
    87-88, 92
Intermediate sanction, 35
Iowa, probation in, 74
Ireland, parole in, 22-23, 41

James, Jesse, 26
Judges' discretion, and
    sentencing, 44
Juvenile justice system, 55-59
    adult criminal justice
        system versus, 58-59
    and change from releas-
        ing juveniles from
        prison at 18th or 21st
        birthday, 57
    and crime rate, 57
    and disposition, 58, 59.
        See also Juvenile
        probation
    history of, 57, 58
    and reform, 59
    and youths tried as
        adults, 55-57
    See also Juvenile
        probation system

Index

Juvenile probation system, 59-67
  and aftercare, 66-67
  and community service, 61-62
  and correctional facilities, 64-66
  and day treatment programs, 63, 66
  and electronic monitoring, 63, 79, 80
  history of, 28, 59-60
  and intensive supervision, 63-64, 77-79
  and low-risk offenders, 61-63
  and mediation, 62
  and probation officers, 60-61, 63
  and recidivism, 63-64
  and restitution, 61-63
  and serious offenders, 60-61, 63
  and wilderness programs, 65-67

Kentucky
  juvenile probation in, 65, 66, 79
  probation in, 73

Lifers, furloughs for, 14-17
Louisiana, boot camp in, 90
Love, Janice, 83-84, 86

Maconochie, Alexander, 22
Mandatory minimum sentences, 28-29, 71
Mark system, 22, 25

Maryland, juvenile probation in, 63, 66
Massachusetts
  halfway houses first established in, 48
  juvenile probation in, 60-61
  probation first used in, 24, 33
Mediation, 62
Michigan
  juvenile probation in, 66-67, 78-79
  minimum sentences in, 86
Middle Ages, 17
Miller, Angela, 15
Minnesota, juvenile probation in, 61
Mississippi, probation in, 79-80
Missouri, probation in, 73
Mosomillo, Anthony, 83
Muckrakers, 27

National Congress of Penitentiary and Reformatory Discipline, 24-25
Newfoundland, parole in, 92-94
New Jersey, probation in, 76
New Mexico, probation in, 74
New York, boot camp in, 90
Nokomis Challenge Program, 66-67
Norfolk Island prison, 22

Oglethorpe, James, 17

Ohio
  boot camp in, 89
  juvenile probation in, 63-64, 78-79
Oklahoma, boot camp in, 90
On Crimes and Punishments (Beccaria), 20
Operation Nite Lite, 60-61
Oregon, juvenile probation in, 79

Parole, 39-53, 83-95
  and boot camps, 48-51, 89-92
  costs of, 51-52
  and curfews, 87
  and day-reporting centers, 92
  definition of, 22-23, 40
  and determinate sentences, 43-44
  and difficulties of life, 45
  and electronic monitoring, 92-93
  evaluation of, 83-95
  federal elimination of, 44
  and furloughs, 14-17, 47
  and good time, 41-42, 45
  and halfway houses, 48
  history of, 22-23, 40-42
  and house arrest, 52
  and indeterminate sentences, 41-42
  and intensive supervision, 52-53, 76, 87-88
  and mandatory minimum sentences, 28-29

Index

and minimum sentences, 86
and monitoring, 51-53
and overcrowded prisons, 51-52
popularity of, 45
and recidivism, 45, 88-94
and release programs, 45-47, 89, 92
and risks, 84-86
and therapy, 92-94
time spent on, 53
and two- and three-strikes laws, 28, 44
and violation of guidelines, 53, 84, 86-87
Parole boards, 42-43, 44, 45, 86
Parole officers, 42, 84-85, 87
caseload of, 51-52
and intensive supervision, 52-53
and monitoring, 51-53
and release from boot camp, 51
and release programs, 45-47
Petersilia, Joan R., 73, 74
Philadelphia system, 20-21, 27
Pillory, 18
Presentence investigation (PSI), 33-34
Prevention programs, 94
Prisons
as correctional institutions, 27-28
cost of, 33, 51

and crime rates, 70-71
history of, 18, 20-22
for juvenile offenders, 57
number of inmates in, 29
parole and overcrowding of, 45, 51-52
probation and overcrowding of, 72
probation versus, 32-33, 70-74
for reform, 20-22, 24, 27
See also Parole
Probation, 31-37, 69-81, 94-95
and classification of offenders, 34-35
and community service, 35-36
cost of, 74
and day-reporting centers, 37, 80-81
definition of, 24
and drug treatment, 76
and electronic monitoring, 79-80
and employment, 76
ending of, 34
evaluation of, 69-81, 94-95
and families, 76
and fines, 35
and first-time offenders, 32, 69, 72
and halfway houses, 48
history of, 23-28, 33
and intensive supervision, 35-37, 74-77
and intermediate sanction, 35

popularity of, 31-32, 33
prison versus, 32-33, 70-74
reasons for, 32-33
and recidivism, 71-74, 75
and restitution, 35
rules of, 34
and women, 31, 32
See also Juvenile probation system
Probation officers, 33-34
for adult criminals, 73, 74
caseloads of, 73
and improving lives of offenders, 34
and intensive supervision, 35-37, 75-76
for juvenile offenders, 60-61, 63
and presentence investigation, 33-34
and terms of probation agreement, 34
Punishments
current view on, 28-29
history of, 17-19, 21-28

Quakers, 20-21, 27

Ranches, 65
Reagan, Ronald, 44
Release programs, 45-47, 89, 92
Restitution, 35, 61-63
Rose, Pete, 39-40, 48

Schneider, William, 55
Sentencing guidelines, 44
Serrano, Jose, 83

Solomon, T. J., 55-57
South Carolina, boot camp
    in, 90
Status offenses, 57

Tabb, Linda, 34
Texas
    boots camp in, 90
    probation in, 74
Therapy, 92-94
Three-strikes laws, 28, 44

"Ticket to leave," 22, 41
Torture, 17
Two-strikes law, 44

Utah, juvenile probation
    in, 62-63

War on Drugs, 44
Washington State
    parole in, 86-87, 89
    probation in, 74

Whipping post, 18
Wiebush, Richard, 78
Wilderness programs,
    65-67
Wisconsin, probation in,
    76-77
Work release, 47, 89, 92

Youth Leadership
    Challenge Program, 66

RICHARD WORTH has 30 years of experience as a writer, trainer, and video producer. He has written more than 25 books. Many of his books are for young adults, on topics that include family living, foreign affairs, biography, and history. He has also written an eight-part radio series on New York mayor Fiorello LaGuardia, which aired on National Public Radio. He presents writing and public speaking seminars for corporate executives.

AUSTIN SARAT is William Nelson Cromwell Professor of Jurisprudence and Political Science at Amherst College, where he also chairs the Department of Law, Jurisprudence and Social Thought. Professor Sarat is the author or editor of 23 books and numerous scholarly articles. Among his books are *Law's Violence*, *Sitting in Judgment: Sentencing the White Collar Criminal*, and *Justice and Injustice in Law and Legal Theory*. He has received many academic awards and held several prestigious fellowships. He is President of the Law & Society Association and Chair of the Working Group on Law, Culture and the Humanities. In addition, he is a nationally recognized teacher and educator whose teaching has been featured in the *New York Times*, on the *Today* show, and on National Public Radio's *Fresh Air*.

Picture Credits